PHYSICS WORLD

9TH

BRIJ BHUSHAN CHAURASIA

ISBN 978-1-63850-751-2

This book is dedicated for all those great teachers who have dedicated themselves to enriching the lives of students.

Contents

CHAPTER ONE

❧

MOTION

A Reference Point is used to describe the location of an object. An object can be referred through many reference points.

Origin – The reference point that is used to describe the location of an object is called Origin.

For Example, a new restaurant is opening shortly at a distance of 5 km north from my house. Here, the house is the reference point that is used for describing where the restaurant is located.

What is motion?

If the location of an object changes with time the object is said to be in motion.

Motion in a Straight Line

Distance – The distance covered by an object is described as the total path length covered by an object between two endpoints.

Distance is a numerical quantity. We do not mention the direction in which an object is travelling while mentioning about the distance covered by that object.

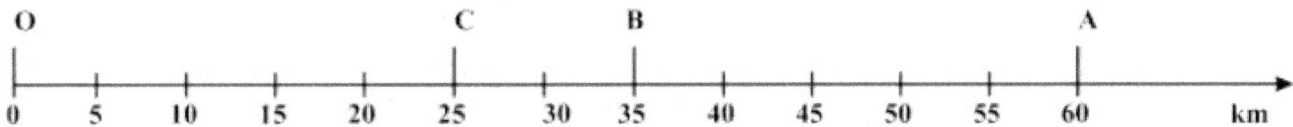

fig-1

Figure 1 – Distance and Displacement

According to the figure 1 given above, if an object moves from point O to point A then total distance travelled by the object is given as 60 km.

Displacement – The shortest possible distance between the initial and final position of an object is called Displacement.

Consider the figure 1 given above, here the shortest distance between O and A is 60 km only. Hence, displacement is 60 km.

Displacement depends upon the direction in which the object is travelling.

Displacement is denoted by Δx.

$\Delta x = xf - x0$

Where,

xf = Final position on the object

x0 = Initial position of the object

Zero Displacement – When the first and last positions of an object are same, the displacement is zero.

For Example, consider the diagrams given below.

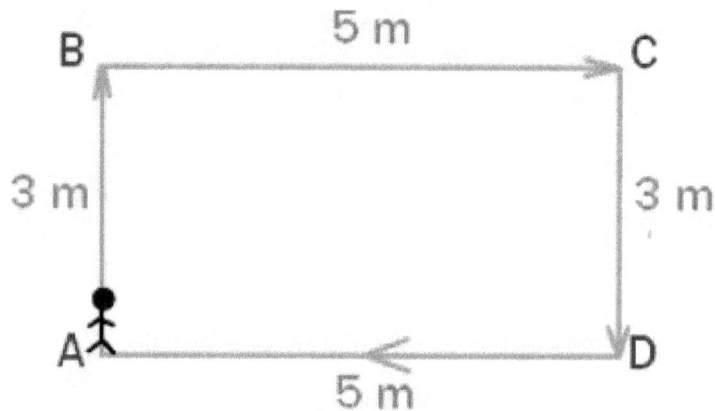

Figure 2 – Example for zero displacement
Displacement at point A = 0 because the shortest distance from A to A is zero.
Negative Displacement and Positive Displacement

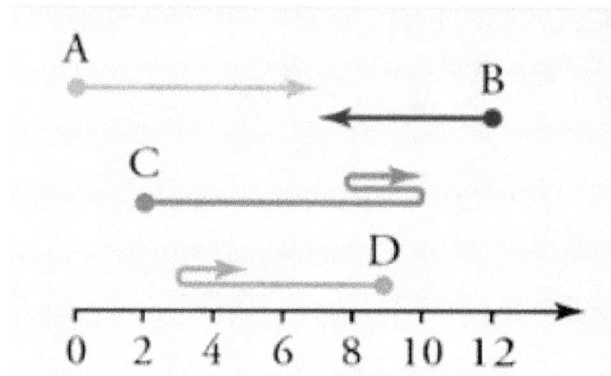

fig--3

Figure 3 – Example for negative and positive displacement
Here, displacement of object B is negative
$\Delta B = Bf - B0 = 7{-}12 = -5$
A negative sign indicates opposite direction here.
Also, displacement of object A is positive
$\Delta A = Af - A0 = 7 - 0 = 7$
What are Scalar and Vector Quantities?
A scalar quantity describes a magnitude or a numerical value.
A vector quantity describes the magnitude as well as the direction.
Hence, distance is a scalar quantity while displacement is a vector quantity.
How is distance different from displacement?
DistanceDisplacement
Distance provides the complete details of the path taken by the object
Displacement does not provide the complete details of the path taken by the object
Distance is always positive
Displacement can be positive, negative or zero
It is a scalar quantity

It is a vector quantity

The distance between two points may not be unique

Displacement between two points is always unique

What is uniform motion?

When an object travels equal distances in equal intervals of time the object is said to have a uniform motion.

What is non-uniform motion?

When an object travels unequal distances in equal intervals of time the object is said to have a non-uniform motion.

Speed of an object is defined as the distance traveled by the object per unit time.

SI Unit: Meter (m)

Symbol of Representation: m/s or ms-1

Speed = Distance/Time

Average Speed – If the motion of the object is non-uniform then we calculate the average speed to signify the rate of motion of that object.

For Example, If an object travels 10m in 3 seconds and 12m in 7 seconds. Then its average speed would be:

Total distance travelled = 10 m + 12 m = 22m

Total Time taken = 3s + 7s = 10s

Average speed = 22/10 = 2.2 m/s

To describe the rate of motion in a direction the term velocity is used. It is defined as the speed of an object in a particular direction.

Velocity = Displacement/Time

SI Unit: Meter (m)

Symbol of Representation: M/s or ms-1

Average Velocity (in case of uniform motion)-

Average Velocity = (Initial Velocity + Final Velocity)/2

Average Velocity (in case of non-uniform motion)-

Average Velocity = Total Displacement / Total Time taken

What are instantaneous speed and instantaneous velocity?

The magnitude of speed or velocity at a particular instance of time is called Instantaneous Speed or Velocity.

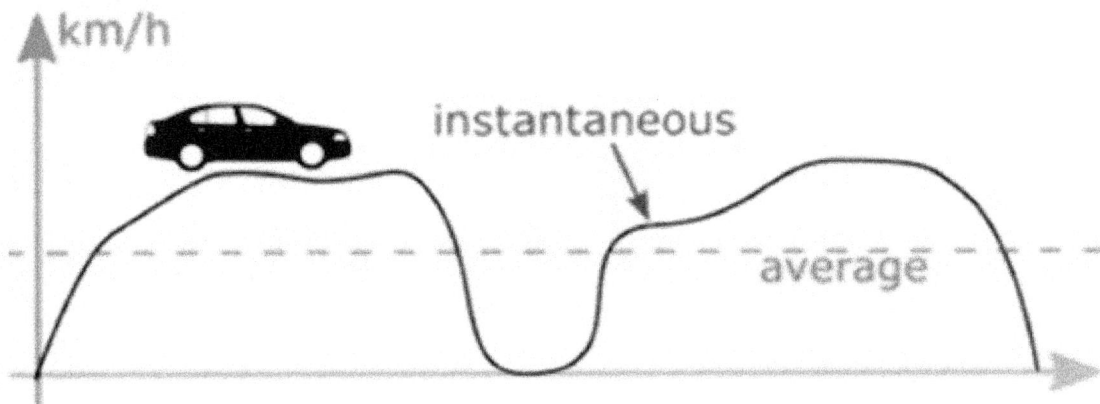

fig--4

Figure 4 - Instantaneous Speed / Velocity

Uniform Motion – In case of uniform motion the velocity of an object remains constant with change in time. Hence, the rate of change of velocity is said to be zero.

Non-uniform Motion – In case of non-uniform motion the velocity of an object changes with time. This rate of change of velocity per unit time is called Acceleration.

Acceleration = Change in velocity/ Time taken

SI Unit: m/s2

Uniform Acceleration – An object is said to have a uniform acceleration if:

It travels along a straight path

Its velocity changes (increases or decreases) by equal amounts in equal time intervals

Non - Uniform Acceleration – An object is said to have a non-uniform acceleration if:

Its velocity changes (increases or decreases) by unequal amounts in unequal time intervals

Acceleration is also a vector quantity. The direction of acceleration is the same if the velocity is increasing in the same direction. Such acceleration is called Positive Acceleration.

The direction of acceleration becomes opposite as that of velocity if velocity is decreasing in a direction. Such acceleration is called Negative Acceleration.

De-acceleration or Retardation – Negative acceleration is also called De-acceleration or Retardation

Graphical Representation of Motion

1. Distance – Time Graph

It represents a change in position of the object with respect to time.

The graph in case the object is stationary (means the distance is constant at all time intervals) – Straight line graph parallel to x = axis

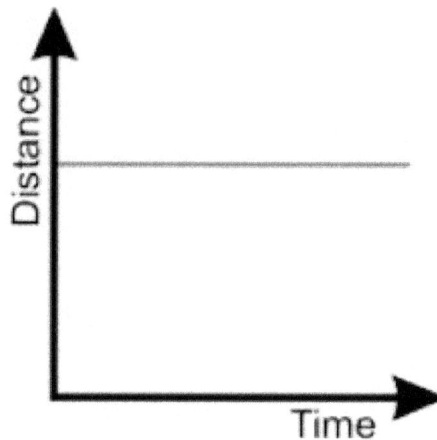

fig--5

Figure 5 - Distance-time Graph in case of Stationary object

The graph in case of uniform motion – Straight line graph

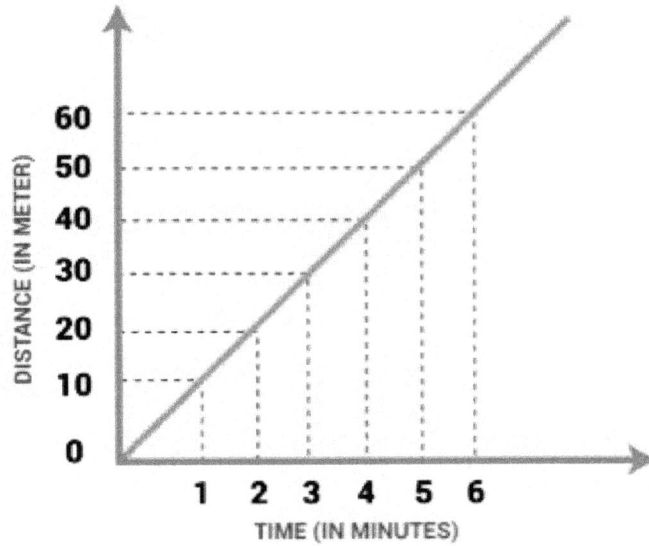

fig--6

Figure 6 - Distance-time Graph in Uniform Motion
The graph in case of non-uniform motion – Graph has different shapes

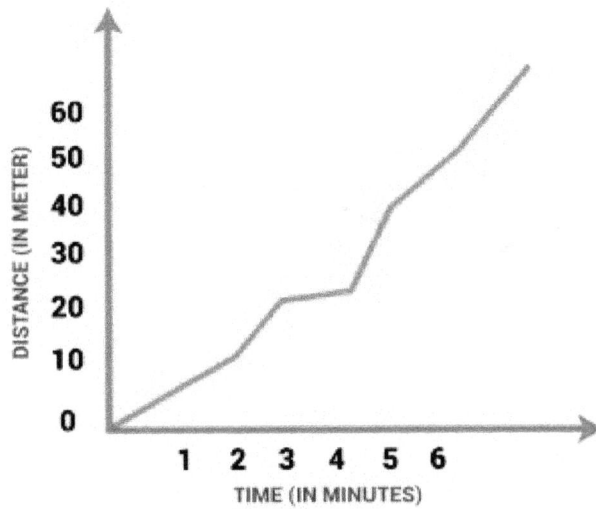

fig--7

Figure 7- Distance-time Graph in Non-Uniform Motion
2. Velocity – Time Graphs
Constant velocity – Straight line graph, velocity is always parallel to the x-axis
Uniform Velocity / Uniform Acceleration – Straight line graph

Velocity

V = constant or uniform

Time

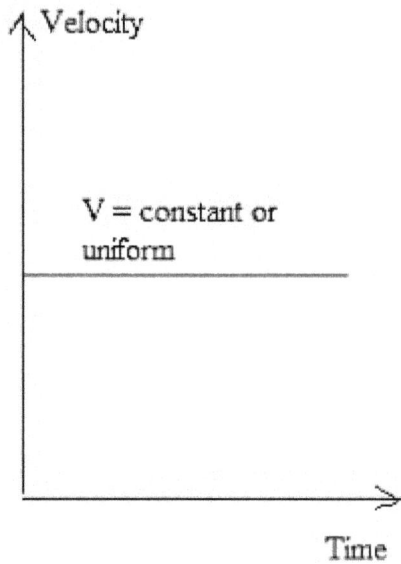

(A) v-t Ccurve for uniform velocity

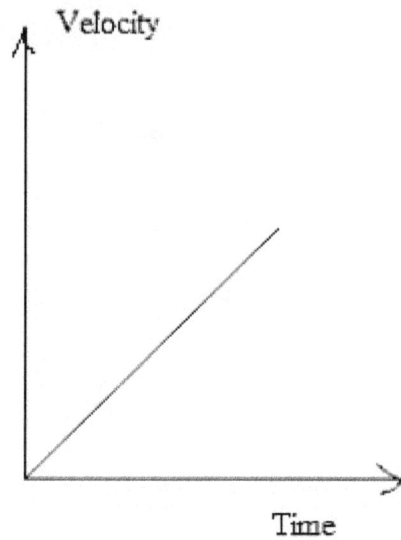

Velocity

Time

(B) v-t curve for uniform acceleration

Non-Uniform Velocity / Non-Uniform Acceleration – Graph can have different shapes

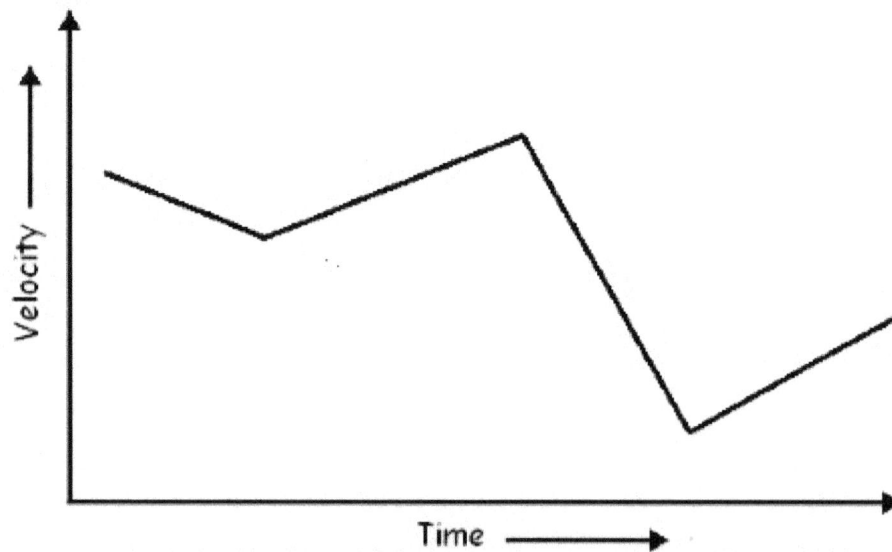

Velocity

Time

Velocity - Time Graph of an object moving with Non-uniform velocity

Calculating Displacement from a Velocity-time Graph

Consider the graph given below. The area under the graph gives the distance traveled between a certain interval of time. Hence, if we want to find out the distance traveled between time interval t1 and t2, we need to calculate the area enclosed by the rectangle ABCD where area (ABCD) = AB * AC.

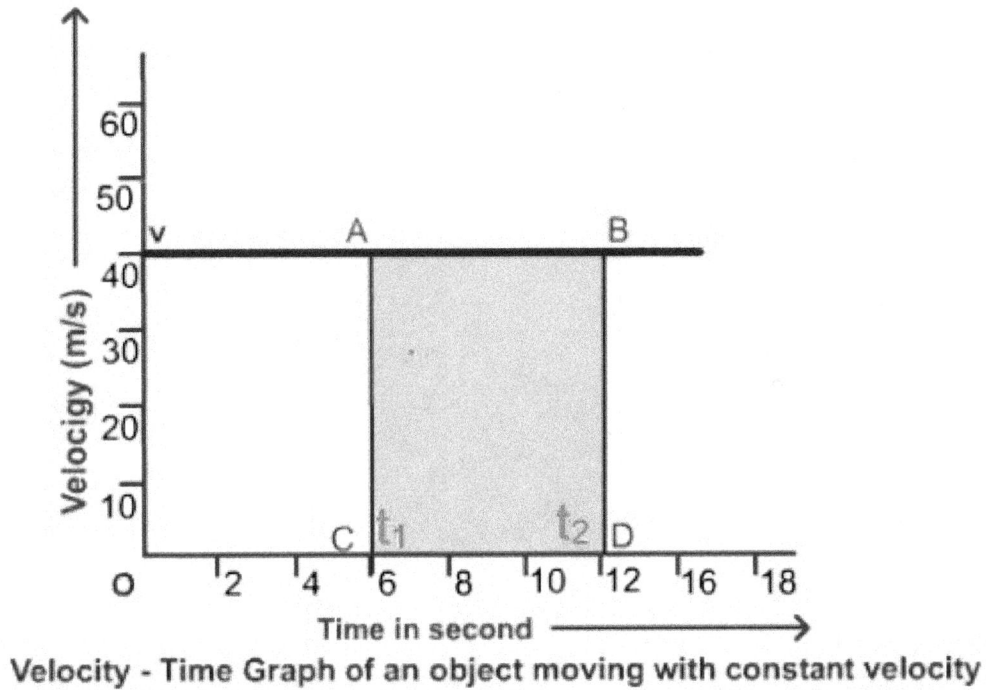

Velocity - Time Graph of an object moving with constant velocity

Similarly, to calculate distance traveled in a time interval in case of uniform acceleration, we need to find out the area under the graph, as shown in the figure below.

To calculate the distance between time intervals t1 and t2 we need to find out area represented by ABED.

Area of ABED = Area of the rectangle ABCD + Area of the triangle ADE = AB × BC + 1/ 2 * (AD × DE)

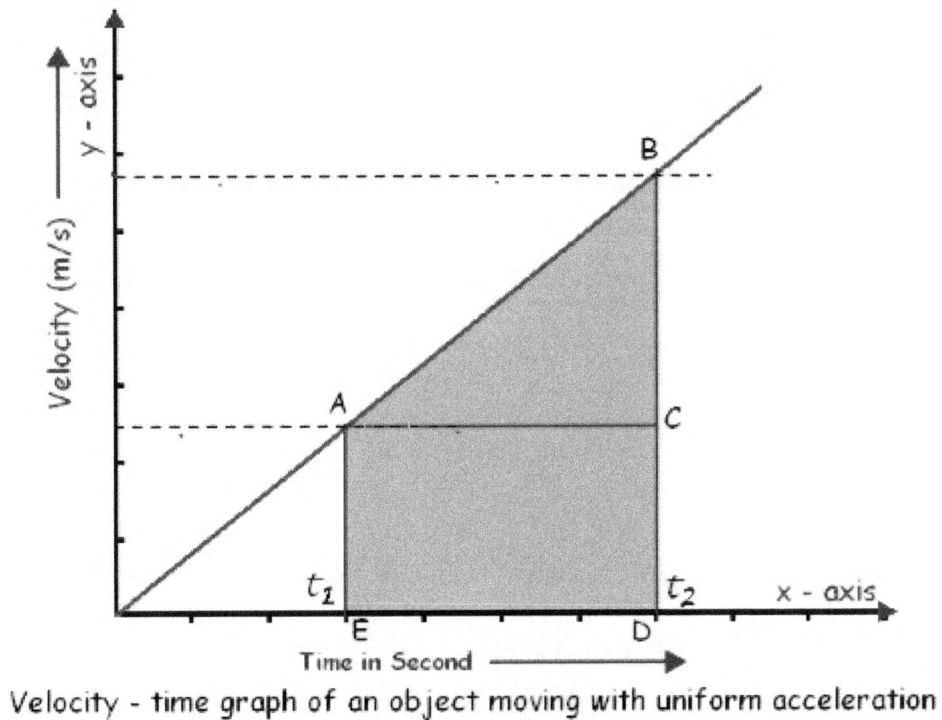

Velocity - time graph of an object moving with uniform acceleration

Equations of Motion

The equations of motion represent the relationship between an object's acceleration, velocity and distance covered if and only if,

The object is moving on a straight path

The object has a uniform acceleration

Three Equations of Motion

1. The Equation for Velocity – Time Relation

$v = u + at$

2. The Equation for Position – Time Relation

$s = ut + 1/2\ at2$

3. The Equation for the Position – Velocity Relation

$2a\ s = v2 – u2$

Where,

u: initial velocity

a: uniform acceleration

t: time

v: final velocity

s: distance traveled in time t

Deriving the Equations of Motion Graphically

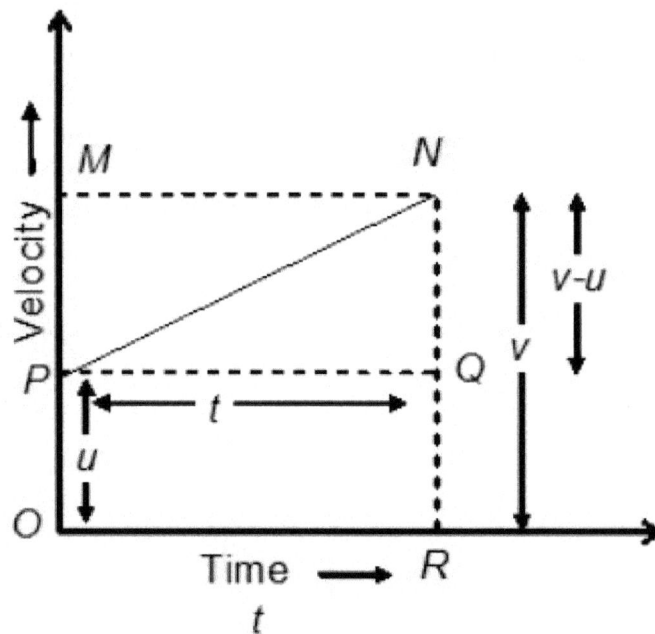

fig--12

Figure 12

Study the graph above. The line segment PN shows the relation between velocity and time.

Initial velocity, u can be derived from velocity at point P or by the line segment OP

Final velocity, v can be derived from velocity at point N or by the line segment NR

Also, NQ = NR – PO = v – u

Time interval, t is represented by OR, where OR = PQ = MN

1. Deriving the Equation for Velocity – Time Relation

Acceleration = Change in velocity / time taken

Acceleration = (final velocity − initial velocity) / time

$a = (v − u)/t$

so, $at = v − u$

$v = u + at$

2. Deriving Equation for Position − Time Relation

We know that, distance travelled by an object = Area under the graph

So, Distance travelled = Area of OPNR = Area of rectangle OPQR + Area of triangle PQN

$s = (OP * OR) + (PQ * QN) / 2$

$s = (u * t) + (t * (v − u) / 2)$

$s = ut + 1/2 \ at2$ [because $at = v − u$]

3. Deriving the Equation for Position − Velocity Relation

We know that, distance travelled by an object = area under the graph

So, s = Area of OPNR = (Sum of parallel sides * height) / 2

$s = ((PO + NR)* PQ)/ 2 = ((v+u) * t)/ 2$

$2s / (v+u) = t$ [equation 1]

Also, we know that, $(v − u)/ a = t$ [equation 2]

On equating equations 1 and 2, we get,

$2s / (v + u) = (v − u)/ a$

$2as = (v + u) (v − u)$

$2 \ a \ s = v2 − u2$

Uniform Circular Motion

If an object moves in a constant velocity along a circular path, the change in velocity occurs due to the change in direction. Therefore, this is an accelerated motion. Consider the figure given below and observe how directions of an object vary at different locations on a circular path.

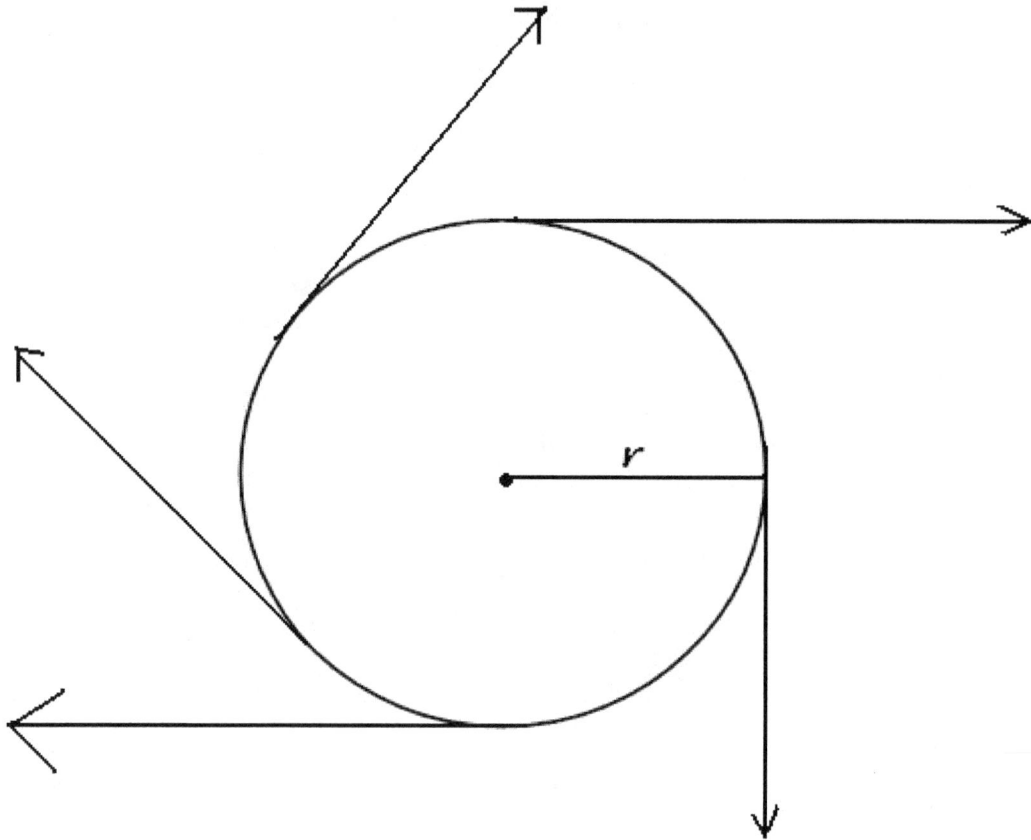

Direction at different point while circular motion

Uniform Circular Motion – When an object travels in a circular path at a uniform speed the object is said to have a uniform circular motion.

Non-Uniform Circular Motion – When an object travels in a circular path at a non-uniform speed the object is said to have a non-uniform circular motion

Examples of uniform circular motion:

The motion of a satellite in its orbit

The motion of planets around the sun

Velocity of Uniform Circular Motion

Velocity = Distance/ Time = Circumference of circle / Time

$v = 2\pi r/ t$

where,

v: velocity of the object

r: radius of the circular path

t: time taken by the object

CHAPTER TWO

FORCE AND LAWS OF MOTION

How does an object start moving?

We need to put some effort to make a stationary object move, For Example, a push, a hit or a pull.

Fig.1- How does an object move

What is a force?

Whenever we push or pull an object a force acts upon them and makes them move from one place to another. Hence, force can –

initiate motion in a motionless object

change (increase or decrease) the velocity of the moving object

alter the direction of a moving object

change the shape and size of an object

Fig.2 - Effects of Force

Balanced and Unbalanced Forces

Balanced Forces –

When equal amount of forces are applied on an object from different directions such that they cancel out each other

They do not change the state of rest or motion of an object

They may change the shape and size of an object

Fig.3- Balanced Forces

Unbalanced Force –

When forces applied to an object are of different magnitude(or not in opposite directions so as to cancel)

They can alter state of rest or motion of an object

They can cause acceleration in an object

They can change the shape and size of an object

Fig.4 – Unbalanced Forces

What is the force of friction?

It is a force extended when two surfaces are in contact with each other. It always acts in a direction opposite to the direction of motion of the object.

Fig. 5 – The force of Friction

First Law of Motion

Galileo's Observation

He observed the motion of objects on an inclined plane.

When a marble is rolled down an inclined plane its velocity increases.

Galileo's Arguments

When a marble is rolled down from the left – It will go up on the opposite side up to the same height at which it is dropped down.

If the inclination of planes is equal – The marble would travel equal distances while climbing up as travelled while rolling down.

If we decrease the angle of inclination of the right plane – The marble would travel further until it reaches its original height.

If the right side plane is made flat – Marble would travel forever to achieve the same height.

Galileo's Inference

We need an unbalanced force to change the motion of the marble but no force is required when the marble is moving uniformly. In other words, objects move at a constant speed if no force acts upon them.

Based on Galileo's ideas Newton presented the three Laws of Motion

First law of motion or The Law of Inertia

Whether an object is moving uniformly on a straight path or is at rest, its state would not change until and unless an external force is applied on to it.

Hence, we can say that objects oppose a change in their state of motion or rest. This tendency of objects to remain in the state of rest or to keep moving uniformly is called Inertia.

Examples of Inertia

We fall back when a vehicle starts moving in the forward direction because our body is in the rest state and it opposes the motion of the vehicle.

We fall forward when brakes are applied in a car because our body opposite the change of state of motion to rest

Inertia and Mass

The inertia of an object is dependent upon its mass.

Lighter objects have less inertia, that is, they can easily change their state of rest or motion.

Heavier objects have large inertia and therefore they show more resistance.

Hence 'Mass' is called a measure of the inertia of an object.

Consider the image given below; it is easier for a person to push the bucket that is empty rather than the one that is filled with sand. This is because the mass of an empty bucket is less than that of the bucket filled with sand.

The Second Law of Motion

The impact produced by a moving object depends upon its mass and velocity.

For Example, a small bullet fired at a high velocity can kill a person.

Momentum – The product of mass and velocity is called Momentum.

It is a vector quantity. Its direction is same as that of the object's velocity.

Denoted by – p

SI unit – kg metre per second

$p = mv$,

where m is the mass of the object,

v is the velocity of the object

The momentum of a stationary object –

Let the mass of a stationary object be 'm',

Let the velocity of a stationary object be 'v',

The stationary object has no velocity, so $v = 0$,

Therefore, $p = m*v = m*0 = 0$

So, the momentum of a stationary object is zero.

We know that the velocity of an object can be changed by applying an unbalanced force on to it. Similarly, the momentum of an object can change by applying an unbalanced force.

According to the second law of motion –

The rate of change of momentum of an object is directly proportional to the applied unbalanced force on the object in the direction of the force.

For Example –

A cricketer when catches a ball pulls his hands in the backward direction to give some time to decrease the velocity of the ball. As the acceleration of the ball decreases the force exerted on catching the moving ball also decreases. If the cricketer would try to stop a moving ball suddenly he would have to apply larger force.

Mathematical Formulation of the Second Law of Motion

Based on the definition of the second law of motion, we can infer that -

Therefore, with help of the second law of motion we can evaluate the amount of force that is being exerted on any object. From the formula stated above, we can see that the force is directly proportional to acceleration. So the acceleration of an object can change depending upon the change in force applied.

Force = ma

SI Unit: kg-ms-2 or N (Newton)

The Third Law of Motion

Action and Reaction Forces

Two forces acting from opposite directions are called Action and Reaction Forces.

For Example, a ball when hits the ground (action) bounces back with a certain force reaction.

Fig. 15 - Action and Reaction Forces

The Third Law of Motion States that –

When an object exerts a force on another object, the second object instantly exerts a force back onto the first object. These forces are always equal in magnitude but opposite in direction. These forces act on two different objects always.

Or in other words, every action has an equal and opposite reaction.

The magnitudes of forces acting upon the objects are same but the acceleration produced in them may or may not be the same because the objects can differ in masses.

For Example, when a bullet is fired from a gun, the gun only moves a little backwards (recoils) while the bullet can travel a large distance. This is because of the difference in the mass of the bullet and the gun.

Conservation of Momentum

As per the law of conservation of momentum, the sum of momenta of two objects before the collision and after collision remains the same given that no external unbalanced force acts upon them. In another way, collision conserves the total momentum of two objects.

Consider the figure given above. Two balls A and B having a certain initial velocities collide with each other. Conditions before the collision-

There is no unbalanced force acting upon them

The initial velocity of A is greater than initial velocity of B

The figure below explains how the momentum of the balls is conserved after the collision.

Fig.18 – Conservation of Momentum

Facts about Conservation Laws

They are considered as the fundamental laws in physics.

They are based on observations and experiments.

They cannot be proved but can be verified or disproved with the help of experiments.

A single experiment is enough to disprove a law, while a single experiment is not enough to prove the same.

It requires a large number of experiments to prove the law.

The law of conservation of momentum was formulated 300 years ago.

There is no single situation present until now that disproves this law.

Other laws of conservation are – law of conservation of energy, the law of conservation of angular momentum, the law of conservation of charge.

A force is a push or a pull.

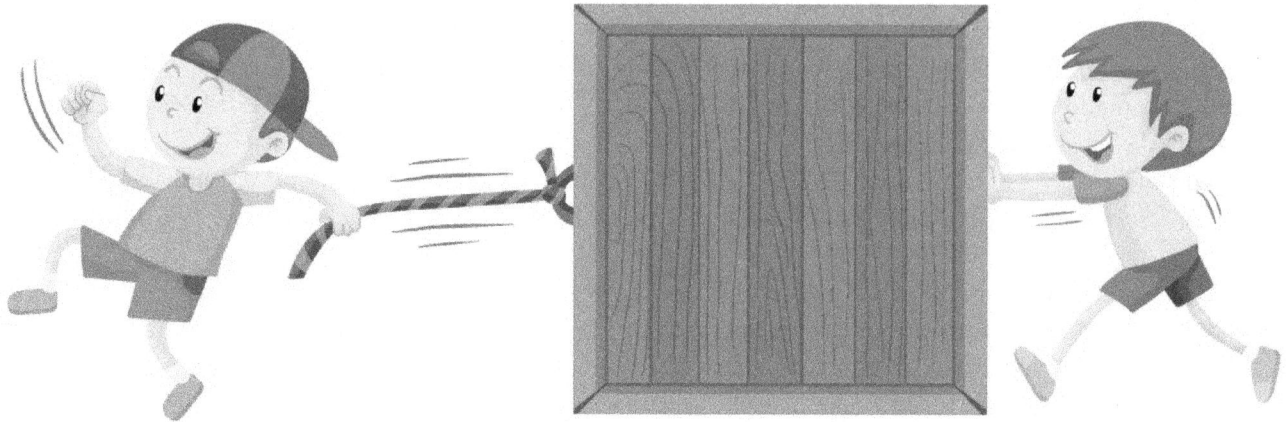

Fig--1 how does an object move

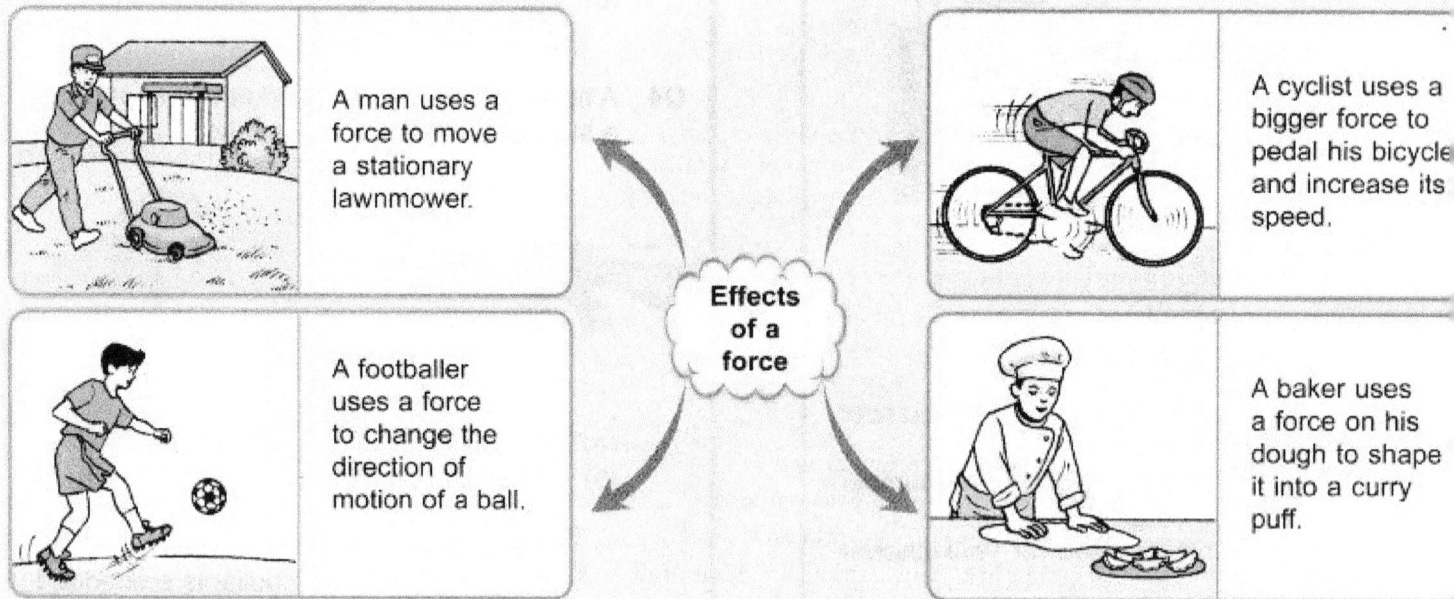

fig--2

Effects of force

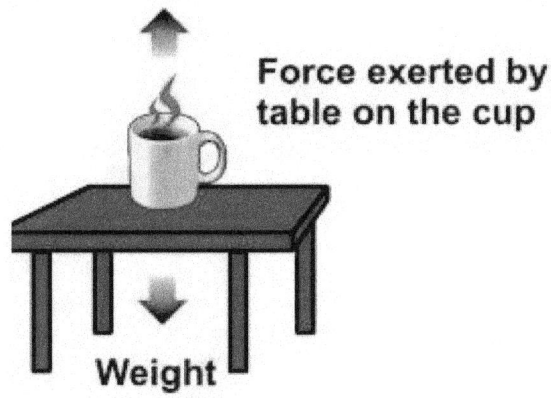

fig--3 balanced force

fig---4

unbalanced force

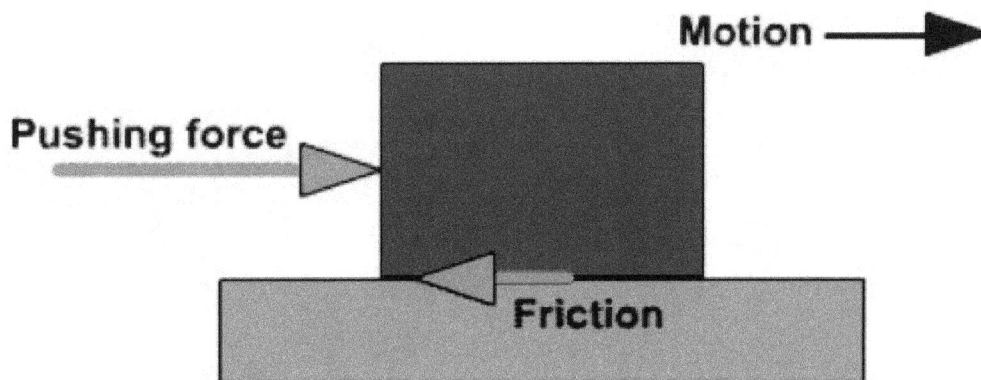

fig--5 the force of friction

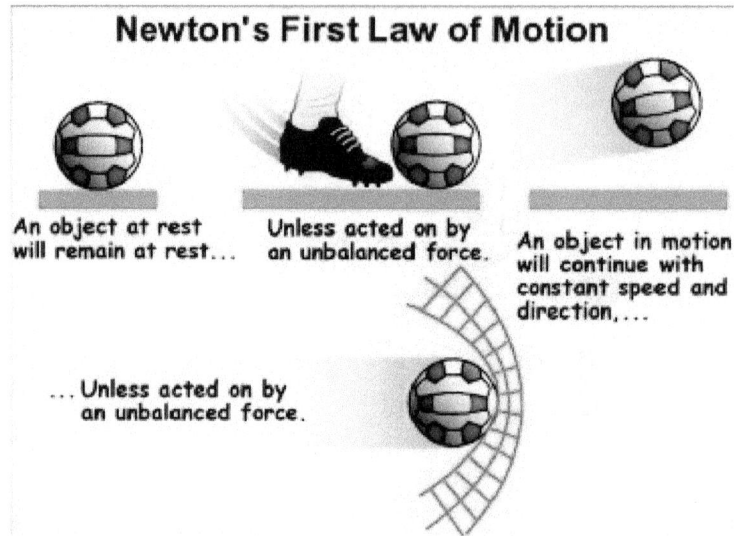

Newton's first law of motion

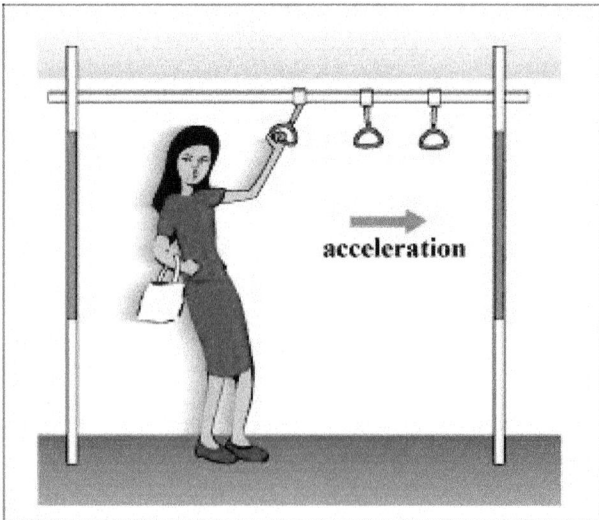

law of inertia

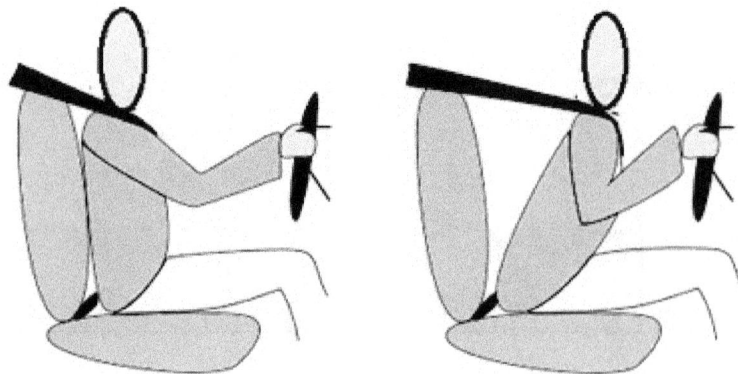

Because of inertia you feel jerk when brakes are applied

Enter Caption

newton's 2nd law of motion

Change in momentum $\propto p2 - p1$

$$\propto mv - mu$$

$$\propto m(v - u)$$

Rate of change of momentum $\propto m(v - u)/t$

Force $\propto m(v - u)/t$

Force $= k\, m(v - u)/t$

Force $= k\, ma$

Force $= ma$

Initial velocity $= u$

Final velocity $= v$

Acceleration $= (v - u)/t$

1 unit of force $= k \times (1\ kg) \times (1\ m\ s^{-2})$

$K = 1$

mathematical formulation

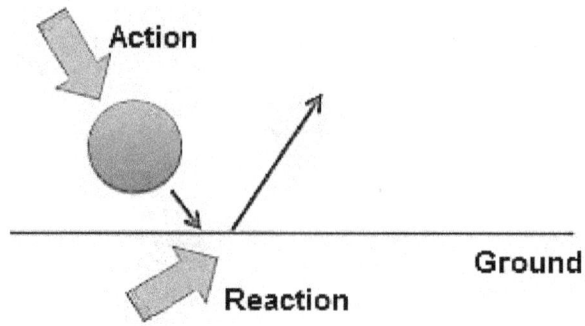

fig--15 newton's 3rd law of motion

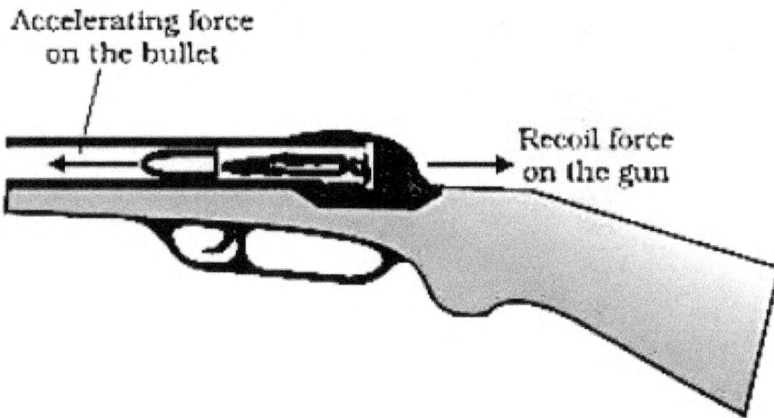

3rd law of motion

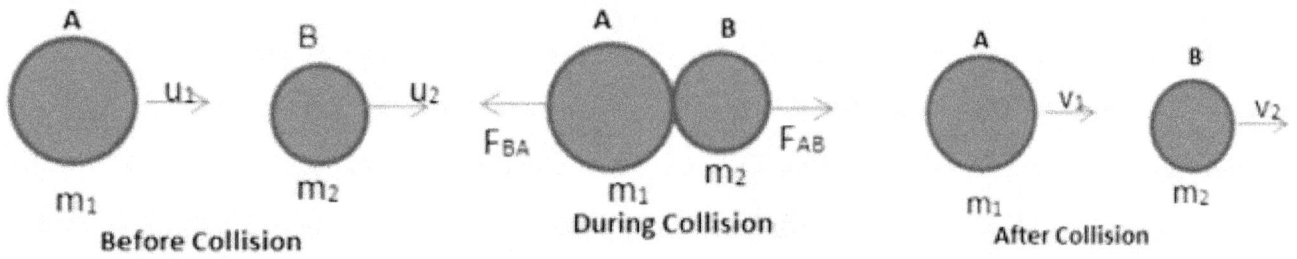

conservation of momentum

The momentum of ball A before collision = $m_A u_A$	According to third law of motion
The momentum of ball A after collision = $m_A v_A$	$F_{AB} = - F_{BA}$ [-ve sign shows opposite force]
The momentum of ball B before collision = $m_B u_B$	$m_A(v_A - u_A)/t = - m_B(v_B - u_B)/t$
The momentum of ball B after collision = $m_B u_B$	$m_A v_A - m_A u_A = - m_B v_B + m_B u_B$
Rate of change of momentum of ball A = $m_A(v_A - u_A)/t$	$m_A v_A + m_B v_B = m_A u_A + m_B u_B$
=Force of action F_{AB}	or
Rate of change of momentum of ball B = $m_B(v_B - u_B)/t$	$m_A u_A + m_B u_B = m_A v_A + m_B v_B$
= Force of reaction F_{BA}	Momentum before collision = Momentum after collision

conservation of momentum

❀

CHAPTER THREE

GRAVITATION

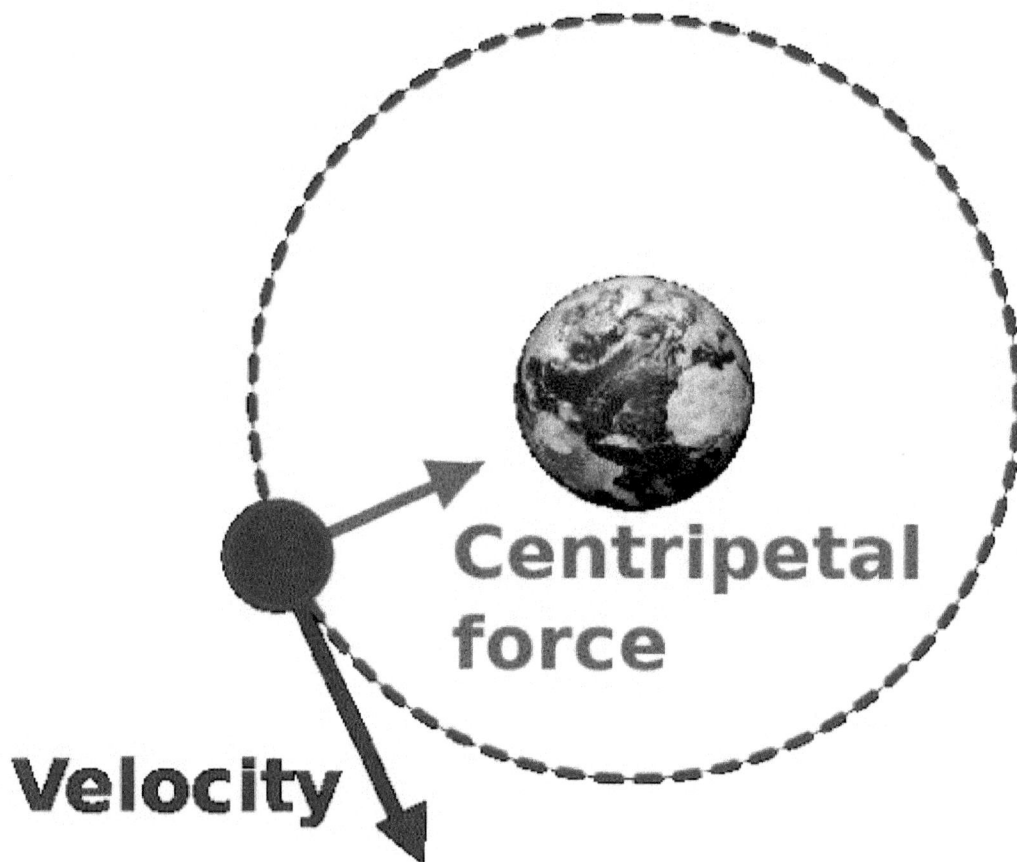

fig--1 centripetal force of earth on moon

What is the Centripetal Force?

We know that an object in circular motion keeps on changing its direction.

Due to this, the velocity of the object also changes.

A force called Centripetal Force acts upon the object that keeps it moving in a circular path.

The centripetal force is exerted from the centre of the path.

Without the Centripetal Force objects cannot move in circular paths, they would always travel straight.

For Example, The rotation of Moon around the Earth is possible because of the centripetal force exerted by Earth.

Figure 1 Centripetal Force of Earth on Moon

Newton's Observations

Why does Apple fall on Earth from a tree? – Because the earth attracts it towards itself.

Can Apple attract the earth? - Yes. It also attracts the earth as per Newton's third law (every action has an equal and opposite reaction). But the mass of the earth is much larger than Apple's mass thus the force applied by Apple appears negligible and Earth never moves towards it.

Newton thus suggested that all objects in this universe attract each other. This force of attraction is called Gravitational Force.

Falling of objects downwards is due to Earth's gravity.

Fig--2 gravitational force of earth

Figure 2 Gravitational Force of Earth
Universal Law of Gravitation by Newton

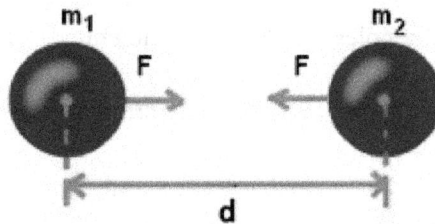

Universal law of gravitation

According to the universal law of gravitation, every object attracts every other object with a force.

This force is directly proportional to the product of their masses.

This force is inversely proportional to the square of distances between them.

Consider the figure given below. It depicts the force of attraction between two objects with masses m1 and m2 respectively that are 'd' distance apart.

The figure below describes how the universal law of gravitation is derived mathematically.

From the above equation we can rewrite them as the following:

If we remove the proportionality we get proportionality constant G as the following:

The above equation is the mathematical representation of Newton's universal Law of gravitation

Hence, $G = Fr2/ m1 m2$

SI Unit: Nm2 kg-2

Value of G = 6.673×10-11 Nm2 kg-2 (was found out by Henry Cavendish (1731- 1810))

The proportionality constant G is also known as the Universal Gravitational Constant

Why we study the universal law of gravitation?

It explains many important phenomena of the universe –

Earth's gravitational force

Why the moon always moves in a circular motion around the earth and the sun

Why all planets revolve around the sun

How the sun and moon can cause tides

Free Fall

Acceleration due to gravity – Whenever an object falls towards the Earth there is an acceleration associated with the movement of the object. This acceleration is called acceleration due to gravity.

Denoted by: g

SI Unit: m s-2

We know that, F= ma

Therefore, F = mg

The following figure demonstrates the mathematical derivation of 'g'

The force (F) of gravitational attraction on a body of mass m due to earth of mass M and radius R is given by

We know from Newton's second law of motion that the force is the product of mass and acceleration.

∴ F = ma

But the acceleration due to gravity is represented by the symbol g. Therefore, we can write

F = mg ..... (2)

From the equation (1) and (2), we get

When body is at a distance 'r' from the centre of the earth then

Value of 'g' may vary at different parts of the earth –

From the equation $g = GM/r2$ it is clear that the value of 'g' depends upon the distance of the object from the earth's centre.

This is because the shape of the earth is not a perfect sphere. It is rather flattened at poles and bulged out at the equator.

Hence, the value of 'g' is greater at the poles and lesser at the equator. However, for our convenience, we take a constant value of 'g' throughout.

We can find the value of acceleration due to gravity by the following –

What is Free Fall?

When an object falls towards the earth due to earth's gravity and no other force is acting upon it, the object is said to be in free fall state. Free falling objects are not even resisted by the air.

g = 9.8 m/s2 is also called the Free-fall Acceleration.

Value of 'g' is same on the earth, so the equations of motion for an object with uniform motion are valid where acceleration 'a' is replaced by 'g', as given under:

v = u + gt

s = ut + (1/2) gt2

2 g s = v2 – u2

Consider the equations of motion given in different scenarios:

When an object at rest falls towards earth – its initial velocity is zero

v = gt

s = t + (1/2) gt2

2 g s = v2

When an object with some initial velocity (u) falls towards earth –

v = u + gt

s = ut + (1/2) gt2

2 g s = v2 – u2

When an object is thrown upwards from earth – the gravitational force acts in opposite direction, hence g is negative

$v = u - gt$

$s = ut - (1/2) gt2$

$-2 g s = v2 – u2$

Difference between Universal gravitational Constant and Acceleration due to Gravity

MassWeight

Mass is defined as the quantity of matter in an object.

The weight of an object is the force by which the gravitational pull of earth attracts the object.

Mass is a scalar quantity

Weight is a vector quantity

The mass of an object is always constant as it depends upon the inertia of the object

The weight of an object can vary at different locations because of change in gravitational force of the earth

Mass can never be zero

Weight can be zero at places there is no gravitational force

Denoted as: m

Denoted as W

$F = mg$

where m = mass of object

a = acceleration due to gravity

Similarly, W is force, so

$W = mg$

SI Unit: kg

SI unit: N

Weight of an object on the Moon

Just like the Earth, the Moon also exerts a force upon objects. Hence, objects on moon also have some weight. The weight will not be same as than on the earth. So, weight on the Moon can be calculated as -

Thrust and Pressure

Thrust

Thrust is perpendicular to surface

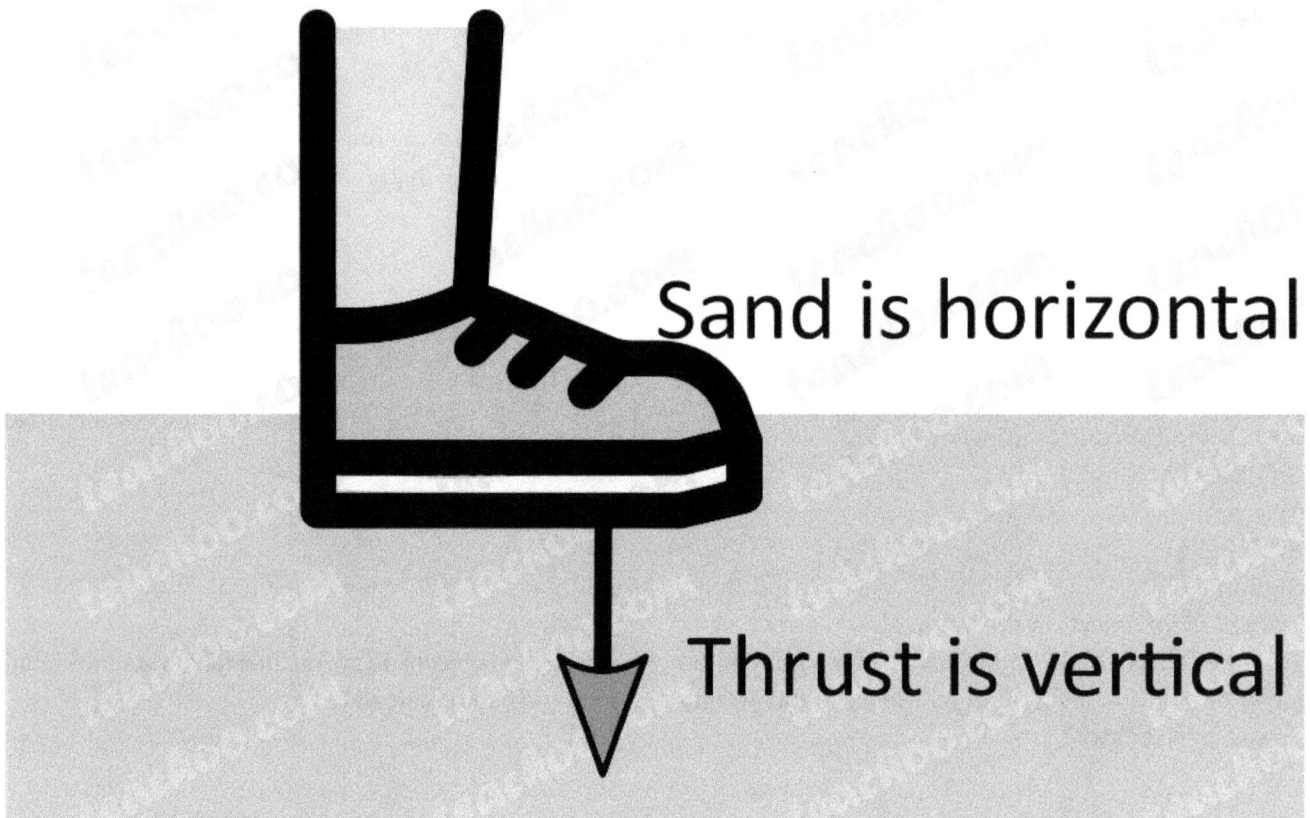

Sand is horizontal

Thrust is vertical

thrust

The force that acts in the perpendicular direction is called thrust.

It is similar to force applied to an object

It is a vector quantity.

Pressure

The force that acts per unit area of the object is pressure.

It is the thrust per unit area.

Pressure is denoted by 'P'

P = thrust/ area = force/ area = F/A

SI unit: N/m2 or Pa (Pascal)

Figure 4 Pressure

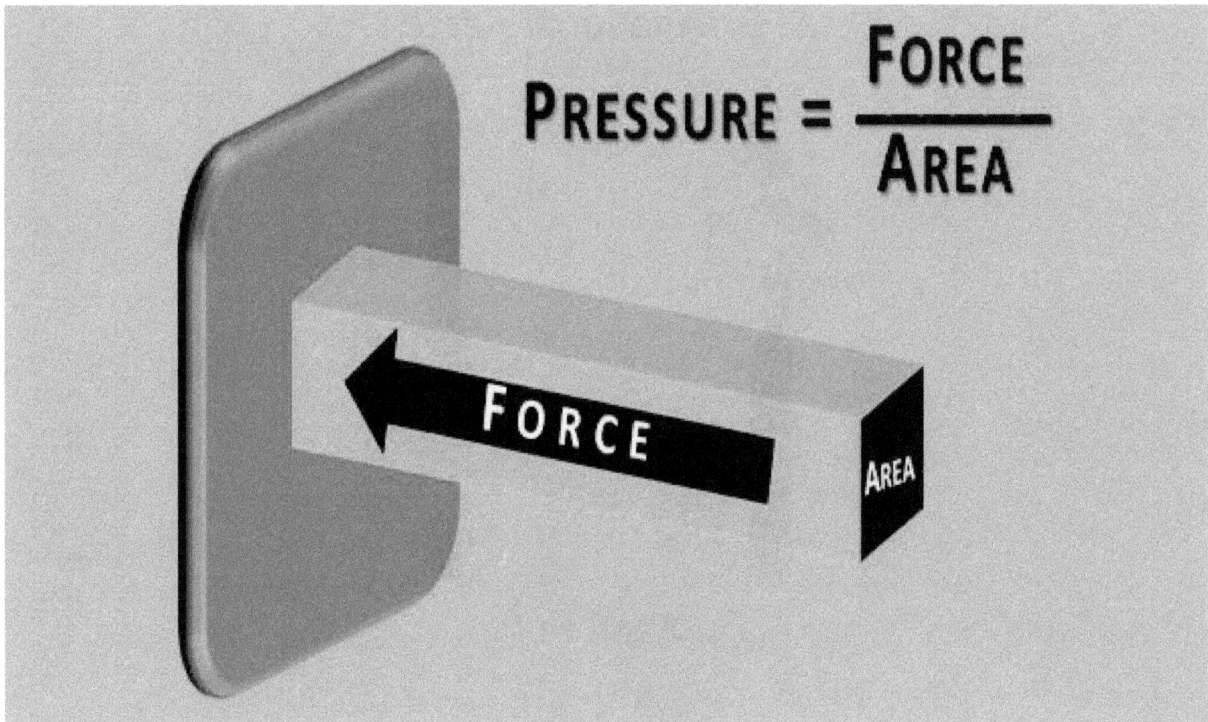

fig--4 pressure

Why do nails have sharp edges?

We know that pressure is inversely proportional to area. As area increases, pressure decreases and vice versa. So, nails' sharp edges make it easier for them to get into the wall because more pressure is exerted on the wall from a single point.

Solids - They exert pressure on the surface because of their weight.

Fluids (gases and liquids) - They also have weight, therefore, they exert pressure on the surface and the walls of the container in which they are put in.

Buoyancy

Whenever an object is immersed in a liquid, the liquid exerts a buoyant force or upthrust in the opposite direction of the gravitational force. This is also called the Force of Buoyancy.

It depends upon the density of the fluid.

Therefore an object is able to float in water when the gravitational force is less than the buoyant force.

Similarly, an object sinks into the water when the gravitational force is larger than the buoyant force.

Figure 5 Buoyancy

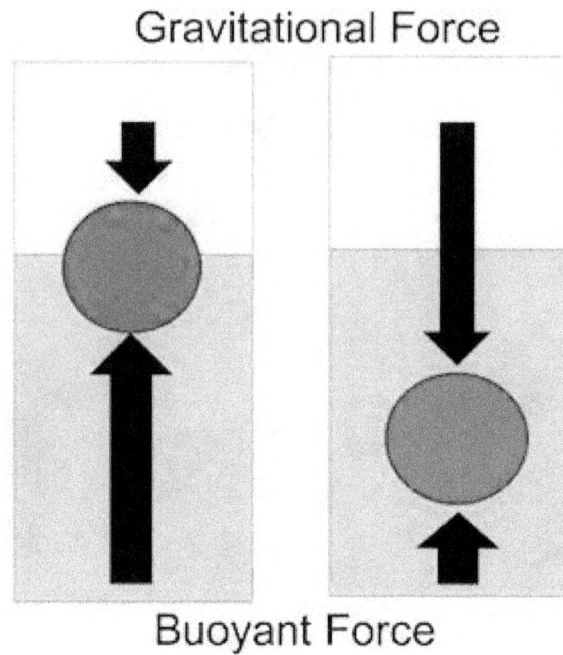

fig--5 buoyancy

Why does an object sink or float on water?

An object can sink or float on water based on its density with respect to water. The density is defined as mass per unit volume.

Objects having a density less than water float in it. For Example, Cork flows in water because its density is lower than that of water.

Objects that have a density higher than water sink in it. For Example, Iron nail sinks in water because the density of iron is more than water's density.

Thus, we can conclude that buoyancy depends upon:

The density of the liquid

The volume of the object (as the volume of object increases, its density decreases and vice-versa)

Archimedes Principle

Understanding
Archimedes'
Principle

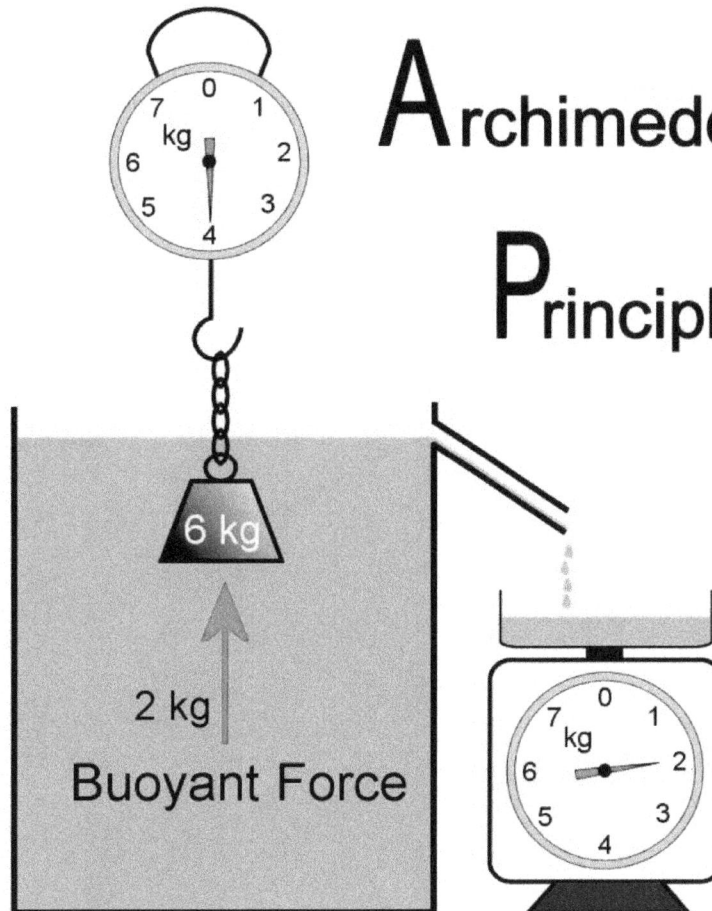

Archimedes priniple

According to the Archimedes principle, whenever an object is immersed in a liquid (fully or partially), the liquid exerts an upward force upon the object. The amount of that force is equivalent to the weight of the liquid displaced by the object.

This means that if the weight of an object is greater than the amount of liquid it displaces, the object will sink into the liquid. However, if the weight of an object is less than the amount of water it displaces, the object will sink.

Submarines have a tank called Buoyancy Tank. Whenever the submarine needs to be taken inside water the tank is filled which thus increases the weight of the submarine. Similarly, when the submarine is to appear above water the tank is emptied and the weight of the submarine becomes lighter and it rises above the water.

Ships are heavier than water but their unique shape gives them a large volume. Their volume is larger than their weight and hence the water displaced by a ship provides it with the right upthrust so that it can float on water.

Applications of Archimedes Principle

In evaluating relative density

In designing ships and submarines

In making lactometers and hydrometers

What is relative density?

When density can be expressed in comparison with water's density it is called Relative Density. It has no unit because it is a ratio of two similar quantities.

Why water is chosen as a reference?

Water is present everywhere on earth so it becomes easier to evaluate the density of a substance in relation to water.

How relative density can be used as a measure to determine in an object will sink or float in water?

Relative Density of an object Float / Sink

Greater than 1 Sink in water

Less than 1 Float in water

CHAPTER FOUR

WORK AND ENERGY

Work

The definition of work done may vary in real life and scientifically. **For Example**, We may consider studying, talking, singing, reading as work but it is not so in the case of science.

Examples of Scientific Work Done are:

- Moving a chair from one location to another
- Lifting a book from the shelf and placing it on a table
- Pushing a pebble lying on the ground.

In all these situations we are applying a force on an object which is then changing the state of rest or motion of the object.

So, we can conclude that work is done if and only if:

- A force is applied to an object.
- If the object is displaced from one point to another point.

These are also called '**Conditions of Work Done**'.

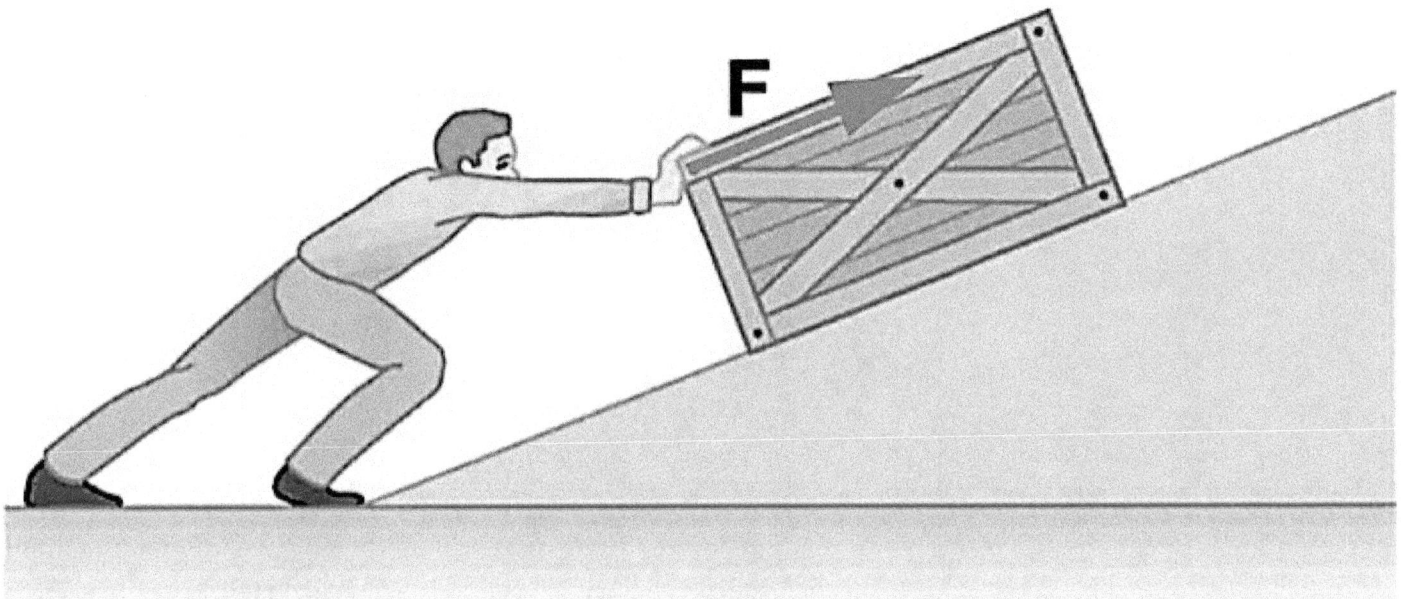

When you play a certain force 'F Newton' on an object and the object moves a distance of ' d meters' in the direction where you applied the force then, the amount of work done can be calculated as:

Work done = Force * Displacement

W = F * d

Definition of Work Done: Work is defined as the product of the force applied on an object and displacement caused due to the applied force in the direction of the force. Work is a scalar quantity. It has no direction of its own but a magnitude.

SI unit of Work: N-m or J (Joule)

What is 1 Joule Work?

A situation where 1 Newton force is applied on an object that can move the object by a distance of 1m in the direction of the applied force, then 1 joule of work is said to be done.

- Depending upon the direction of displacement and force applied the nature of work done may vary. Consider the table given below:

The direction of Displacement
Work Done
Nature of Work Done
Angle between Force applied and Displacement occurred
Same as the direction of Force
W = F * d
Positive
0°(Force and Displacement are Parallel to each other)
Opposite as direction of Force
W = -F * d
Negative
180°
No change in position
W = F * 0 = 0
Zero
90°

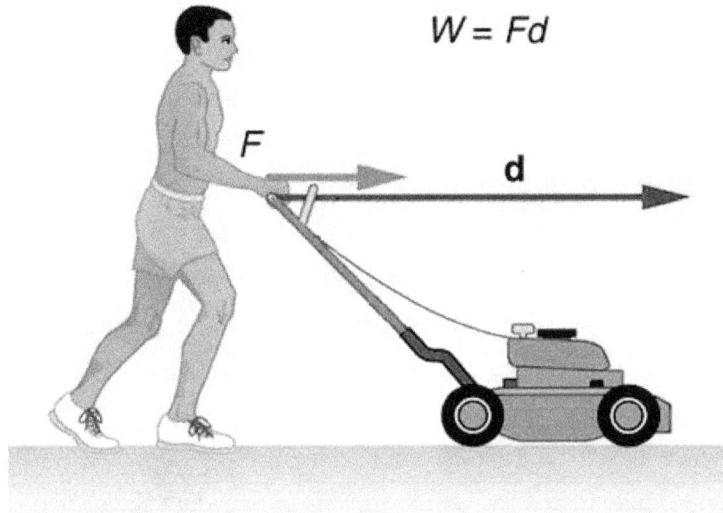

$$W = Fd$$

Positive Work Done

Negative Work Done

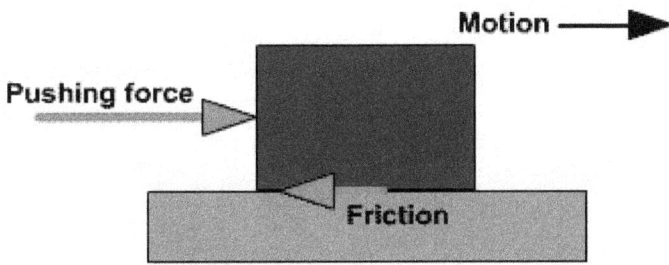

Zero   Work   Done

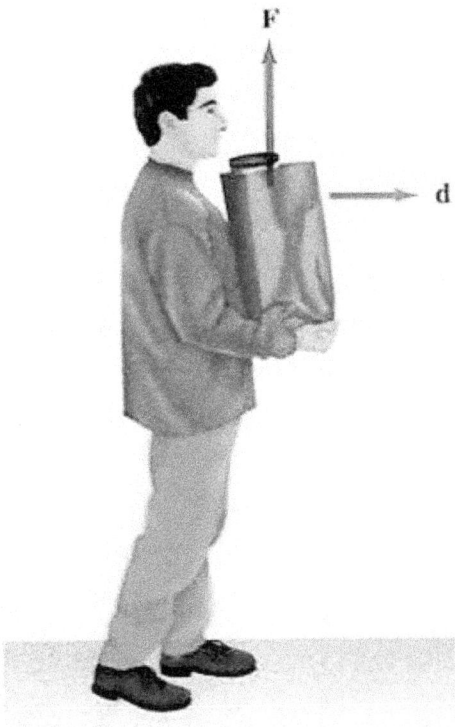

Energy

Any object that is capable of doing work processes some energy. The object can gain or lose energy depending upon the work done. If an object does some work it loses its energy and if some work is done on an object it gains energy.

Different forms of energies

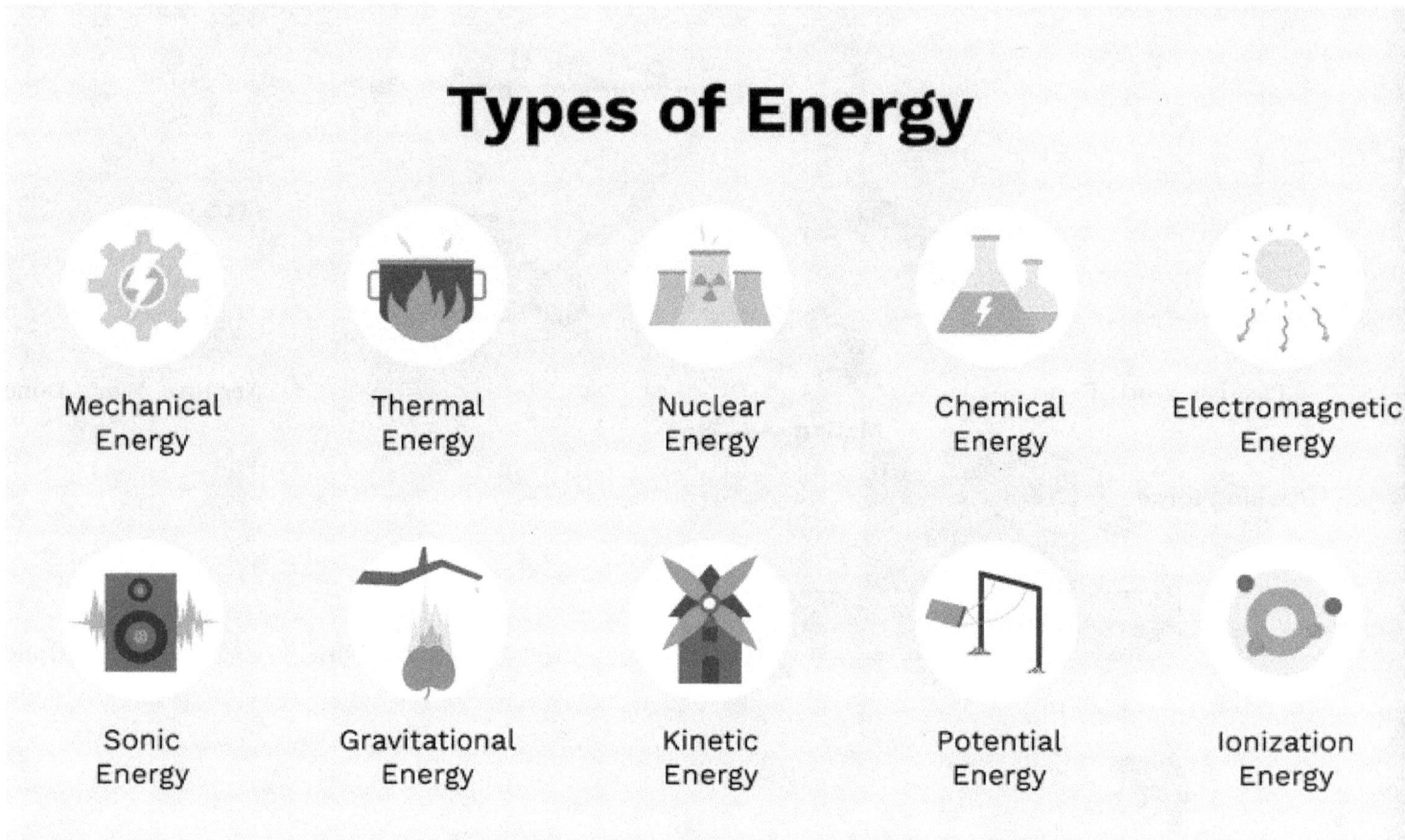

Types of Energy

Mechanical Energy	Thermal Energy	Nuclear Energy	Chemical Energy	Electromagnetic Energy
Sonic Energy	Gravitational Energy	Kinetic Energy	Potential Energy	Ionization Energy

Kinetic Energy

Every moving object possesses some energy called **Kinetic Energy**. As the speed of the object increases so is its kinetic energy.

Formula for Kinetic Energy

$\therefore$ Work done $\rightarrow$ $W = F \times s$ ... (i)

due to force the velocity changes to v, and the acceleration produced is a

$\therefore$ relationship between v, u, a and $s = v^2 - u^2 = 2as$

$\therefore$
$$s = \frac{v^2 - u^2}{2a}$$ ... (ii)

$$F = ma$$ ... (iii)

Substitute (ii) and (iii) in (i) we get

$$W = F \times s$$

$$= ma \times \frac{v^2 - u^2}{2a}$$

$$W = \frac{1}{2} m (v^2 - u^2)$$

if $u = 0$, (object starts at rest)

$\therefore$
$$W = \frac{1}{2} mv^2$$

Work done = Change in kinetic energy

$\therefore$
$$\boxed{E_k = \frac{1}{2} mv^2}$$

Potential Energy

Every object possesses some energy called **Potential Energy**. An object when gains energy may store it in itself as potential energy.

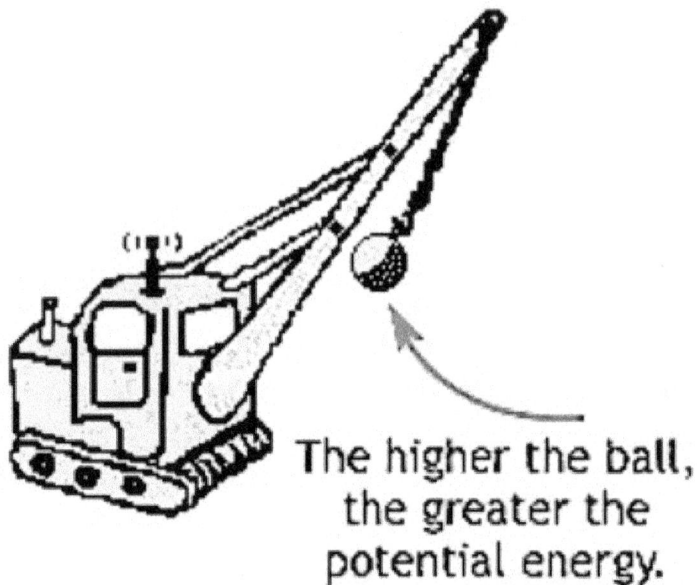

The more the bow is pulled back, the greater the potential energy.

The higher the ball, the greater the potential energy.

We know that when an object rises above the ground some work is done against gravity. Since work is done on the object, the object would gain some energy. The energy that the object gains at a height is called **Gravitational Potential Energy**. It is defined as the amount of work done required in raising an object above the ground up to a certain point against the gravity

Consider the example given below,

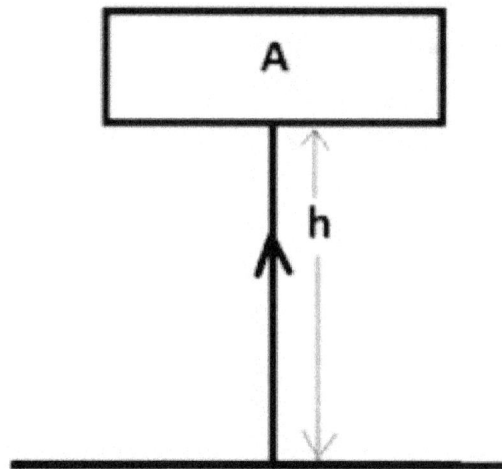

An object 'A' having mass 'm' is raised by height 'h' above the ground. Let us calculate the potential energy of object A at height 'h':

We know that,

$W = F * d = F * h$ (height)

And $F = m * g$ (because the force is applied against gravity)

So, $W = m * g * h$

Hence potential energy of object A, $\mathbf{Ep = m * g * h}$

- Gravitational potential energy does not get affected due to the path taken by the object to reach a certain height.

Other forms of Energies:

- **Mechanical Energy–** It is the sum of kinetic and potential energy of an object. Therefore, it is the energy obtained by an object due to motion or by the virtue of its location. **Example**, a bicycle climbing a hill possesses kinetic energy as well as potential energy.
- **Heat Energy–** It is the energy obtained by an object due to its temperature. It is also called **Thermal Energy**. **Example**, energy possessed by a hot cup.
- **Chemical Energy–** It is the energy accumulated in the bonds of chemical compounds. Chemical energy is released at the time of chemical reactions. **Example**, energy possessed by natural gas and biomass.
- **Electrical Energy–** It is kind of kinetic energy caused due to the motion of electrons. It depends upon the speed of electrons. As the speed increases so does the electrical energy. **Example**, electricity produced by a battery, lightning at thunderstorms
- **Light Energy –** It is the energy due to light or electromagnetic waves. It is also called as **Radiant Energy**or **Electromagnetic Energy**. **Example**, energy from the sun
- **Nuclear Energy–** It is the energy present in the nucleus of an atom. Nuclear energy releases when the nucleus combines or separate. Therefore, we can say that every atom in this universe comprises of nucleus energy. **Example**, uranium is a radioactive metal capable of producing nuclear energy in nuclear power plants
- **Sonic Energy–** It is the energy produced by a substance as it vibrates. This energy flows through the substance in the form of sound waves. **Example**, music instruments produce sound energy
- **Ionization Energy–** It is the energy that binds electrons with its nucleus. It is thus the amount of energy required to remove one electron completely from its atom (called **First Ionization Energy**). Subsequently, the ionization energy increases as we remove the second electron from the atom (called **Second Ionization Energy**).

- One form of energy can be transformed into other forms of energy.

Law of Conservation of Energy

According to the law of conservation of energy, the total amount of energy before and after transformation remains the same.

Consider the following example where an object of mass 'm' is made to fall freely from a height 'h'.

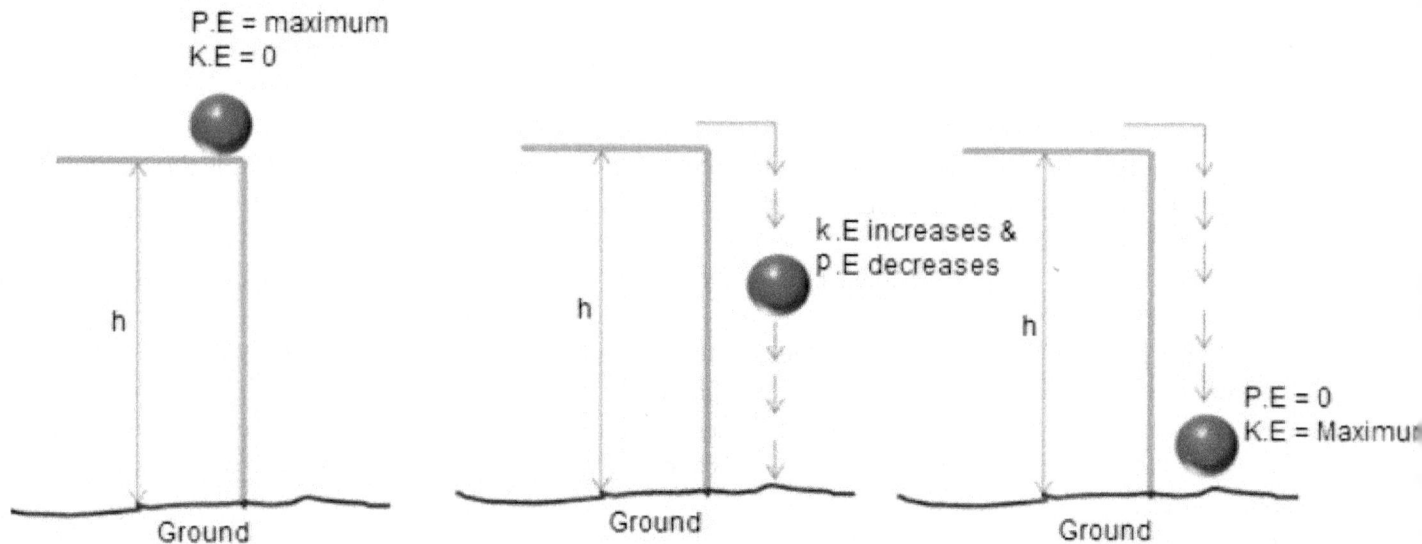

InstantHeight at an instantKinetic EnergyPotential EnergySum of KE + PE = ME1 Height = h0 (velocity is 0)$mgh0 + mgh$2Height = k$(1/2)$ $mv1^2$(velocity = v1)$mgk$$(1/2)$ $mv_1^2 + mgk$3Height = 0$(1/2)$ $mv2^2$(velocity = v2)0$(1/2)$ $mv_2^2 + 0$

We can see that the sum of kinetic energy and potential energy at every instant is constant. Hence, we can say the **energy is conserved during transformation.**

Power– The rate of doing work is defined as **Power.**

Power = Work Done / Time

P = W/ t

SI Unit: W (Watt) or J/s

1 kilowatt = 1000 watts

1 kW = 1000 W

1 W = 1000 J s^{-1}

Average Power = Total Energy Consumed / Total Time taken

Commercial Unit of Power

We cannot use Joule to measure power commercially. Instead, we use kilowatt-hour (kWh).

Commercial unit of energy = 1 kilowatt hour (kwh)

∴ 1 kWh = 1 kilowatt × 1 hour

= 1000 watt × 3600 seconds

= 3600000 Joule (watt × second)

1 kWh = 3.6 × 10^{6}J.

∴ 1 kWh = 1 unit

The energy used in one hour at the rate of 1 kW is called 1 kWh.

✿

CHAPTER FIVE

SOUND

Sound energy is a form of energy because of which our ears are able to hear something.

One cannot create sound or destroy it. But one can transform one form of energy into sound energy. For instance, when a cell phone rings, the sound is produced by converting electrical energy into sound energy.

How is a sound produced?

A sound is produced when an object vibrates, that is they move in a 'to-and-fro' motion.

For instance,

When we strike a tuning fork or a stretched rubber band, it vibrates and produces sound.

The human voice is produced because of the vibration of the vocal cords.

String instruments produce sound as their strings vibrate.

When a bird flaps its wings a sound is produced.

A flute produces sound because the air column of the flute vibrates as air passes through it.

How does sound travel?

In order to propagate, sound requires a medium through which it can travel. This medium could be a gas, liquid or solid.

Sound propagates in a medium as the particles of the medium vibrate from a starting point. This means that sound always has a starting point and an ending point.

For instance, while you talk to a friend, as you speak, the particles in the air get displaced due to the pressure caused by the sound you produce. They then displace the adjacent particles and so on. In this way, sound travels from your place to your friend's ears.

Therefore, we can say that the particles of a medium do not travel from one point one another in order to propagate sound. Sound propagates because of the disturbance caused by a source of sound in the medium.

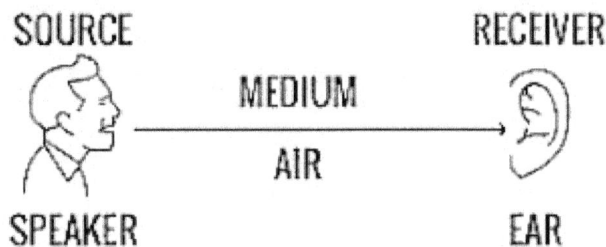

sound travel through a medium

Sound travels through a medium

What is a wave?

A wave is a disturbance produced in a medium as the particles of the medium vibrate.

The particles produce motion in each other without moving forward or backwards.

This leads to the propagation of sound.

Hence sound is often called a Wave.

How can sound travel through air?

When an object vibrates in the air or produces a sound, some regions of high pressure are created in front of it. These are called the Regions of Compression. These regions of compression move forward in the medium as particles exert pressure on their adjacent particles.

WIth alternate regions of compression, there are also regions of low pressure that are in its front. Thes are called Regions of Rarefaction.

As the object would move forwards and backwards consecutively producing sound, the series of compressions and rarefactions will be created. This will allow sound to move through air or any other medium as well.

If the medium is dense the pressure exerted on the particles will be more in order to propagate the sound and vice versa.

Therefore, we can also say that propagation of sound is all about change in the pressure of the medium.

Sound wave causing compression (C) and refraction (R)

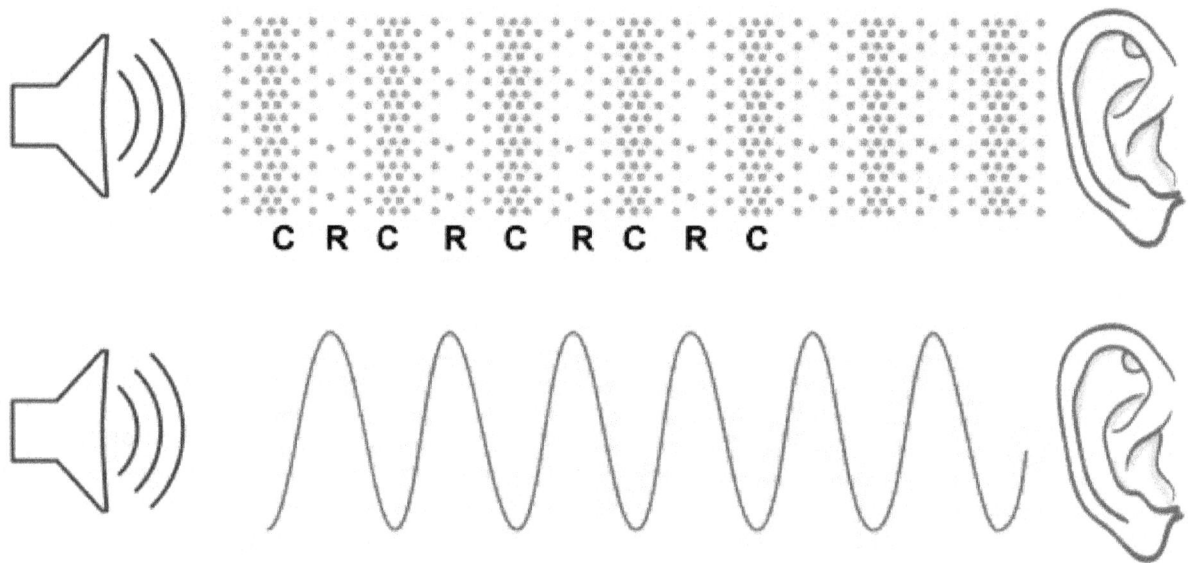

compression and rarefraction

What are mechanical waves?

A wave that is produced when objects of the medium oscillate is called Mechanical Wave. The sound waves are therefore, mechanical waves.

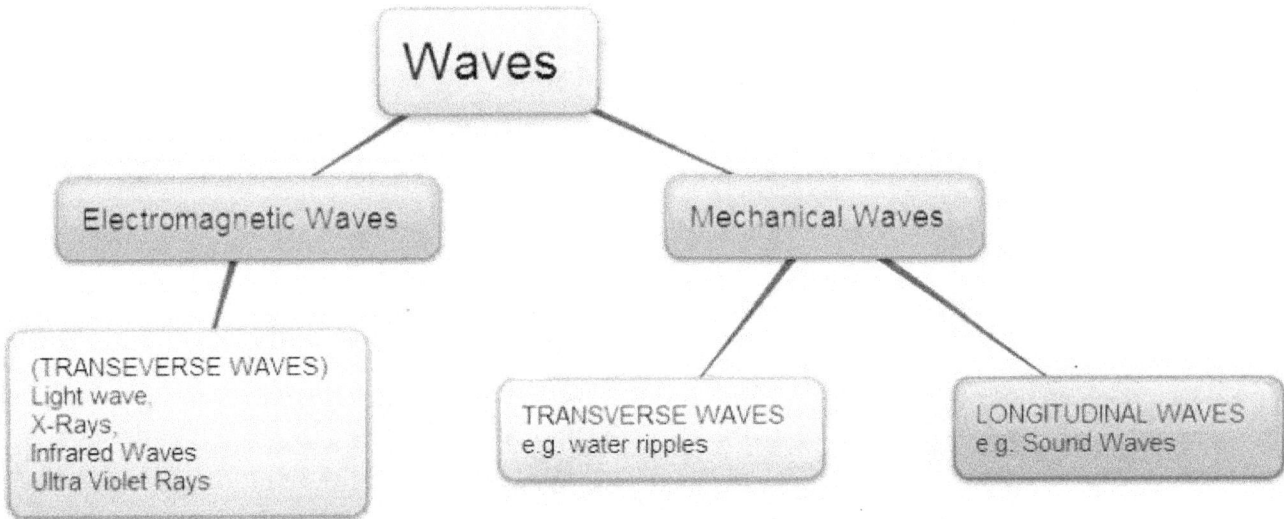

types of wave

Types of Waves

Sound cannot travel through the vacuum as it always needs a medium to propagate. The vacuum contains no air hence no particles can propagate sound.

Longitudinal waves - Any wave that vibrates in the direction of the motion is called a Longitudinal Wave. Sound waves are longitudinal because the particles of the medium vibrate in the direction which is parallel to the direction of the propagation of the sound waves.The particles in the medium oscillate to and fro in the case of longitudinal waves.

Transverse Waves - A transverse wave is produced when the particles of the medium oscillate in a direction which is perpendicular to the direction of the propagation of the wave. The particles in a transverse wave oscillate in an up and down motion. For Example, light waves are transverse in nature.

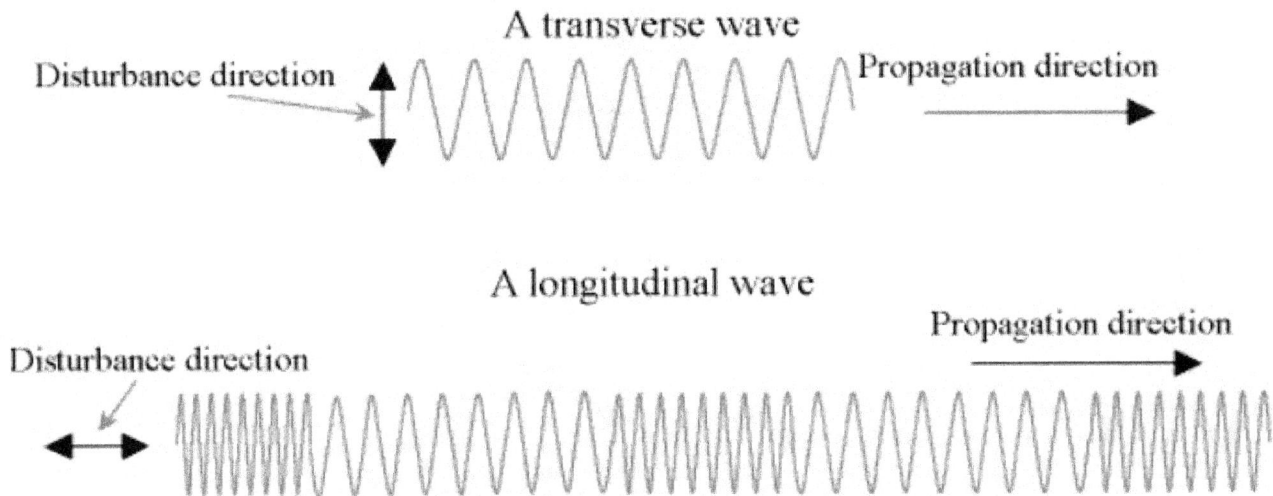

transverse and longitudinal wave

Longitudinal vs. Transverse Waves
A sound wave is characterized by three factors:
Amplitude
Frequency
Speed

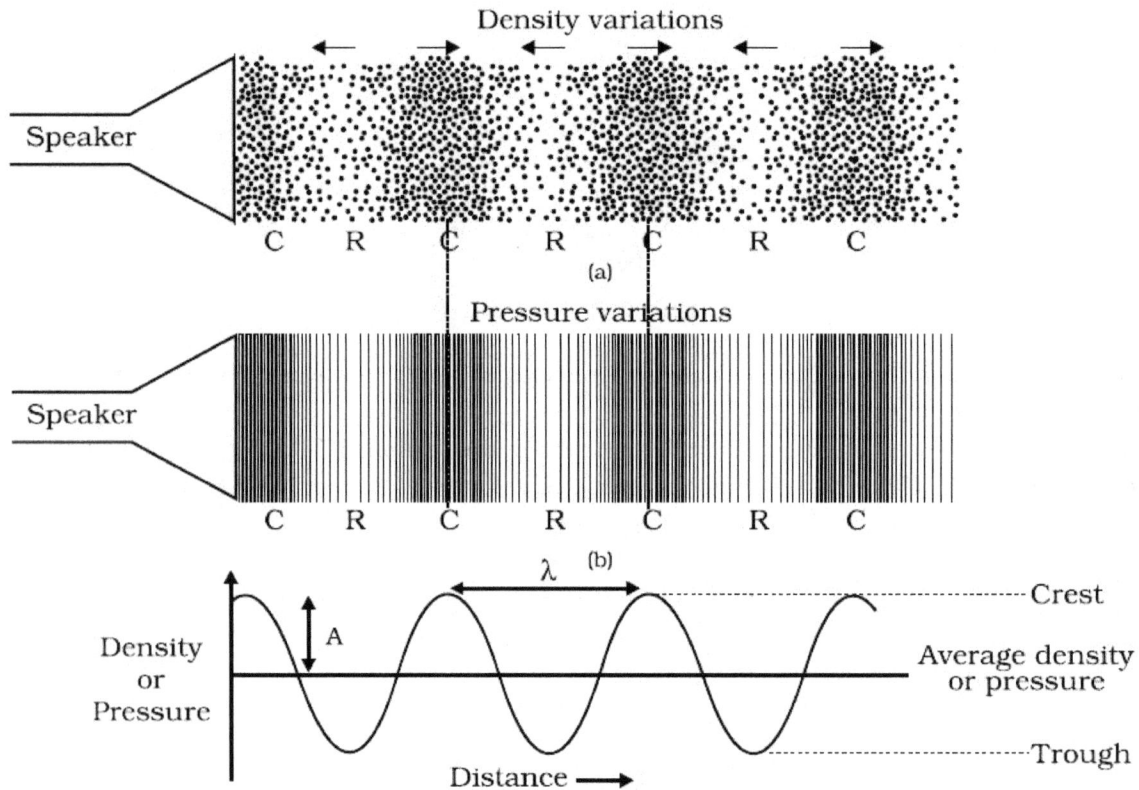

Density variations

Speaker

C   R   C   R   C   R   C

(a)

Pressure variations

Speaker

C   R   C   R   C   R   C

λ (b)

Density
or
Pressure

A

Average density
or pressure

Crest

Trough

Distance

characterists of sound

Characteristics of Sound
Compression (C)
The compression region is represented by the upper part of the wave curve.
It is a region where particles cluster together.
The density, as well as pressure, is always high in this region.
Refraction (R)
A refraction is represented by the lower part of the wave curve.
It is a region where the particles separate out.
Refraction region always has lower pressure.
Crest
It is the peak of the curve
Trough
It is the crust of the curve
Wavelength (λ)

The distance between two consecutive compressions or refractions is called Wavelength.

SI unit: metre (m)

Frequency (f)

The number of oscillations per unit time is called the Frequency of a Wave (Number of compressions + the number of refractions per unit time)

SI unit: Hertz (Hz)

Time Period (T)

The time taken between two consecutive compressions or refractions to cross a fixed point is called Time Period of the Wave.

In other words, the time taken for one complete oscillation through a medium is called a Time Period.

SI unit: second (s)

The relationship between frequency and time period

$f = 1/T$

Pitch

Pitch of a sound depends upon:

1. the frequency of the sound

2. size of the object producing the sound

3. type of the object producing the sound

Amplitude

The value of the maximum or minimum disturbance caused in the medium is called the Amplitude of the Sound.

Amplitude defines if the sound is loud or soft.

Timber

The timbre or quality of sound is a characteristic with which we can differentiate between different sounds even if they have same pitch and amplitude.

Tone

The sound which has single frequency throughout is called a Tone.

Note

A sound with more than one frequency is called a Note. It is pleasant to listen

Noise

It is an unpleasant sound.

Music

It is a sound which is pleasant and has rich quality

The Speed of sound (v)

The distance by which a compression or refraction of a wave travels per unit time is called as Sound's Speed.

SI unit: metres/seconds

$v = $ wavelength $/$ time $= \lambda/T = \lambda*F$

Speed of Sound in air = 333 m/s

Intensity

The amount of sound energy that passes through a unit area per second is called its intensity

Loudness

It is how our ears respond to a sound.

Two sounds with same intensity can vary in loudness only because we can detect one sound easier than the other.

Sound cannot travel at the same speed in different mediums. The speed of sound in a medium is affected by three things:

The density of the medium. For instance, speed of sound is the maximum through solids

The temperature of the medium. As the temperature increases, the sound propagates easily.

Humidity in the air also affects the travel of sound. As the humidity increases, so does the propagation of sound.

What is a sonic boom?

When an object travels in the air with a speed greater than that of the sound, it produces a sound with high energy. This energy is loud enough that it can break glasses or damage the buildings. The sound produced is similar to the sound of an explosion or thunderclap.

These objects exert a large amount of pressure on the air which causes the production of shock waves in the air. These shock waves produce extremely large and loud sound waves which are called Sonic booms.

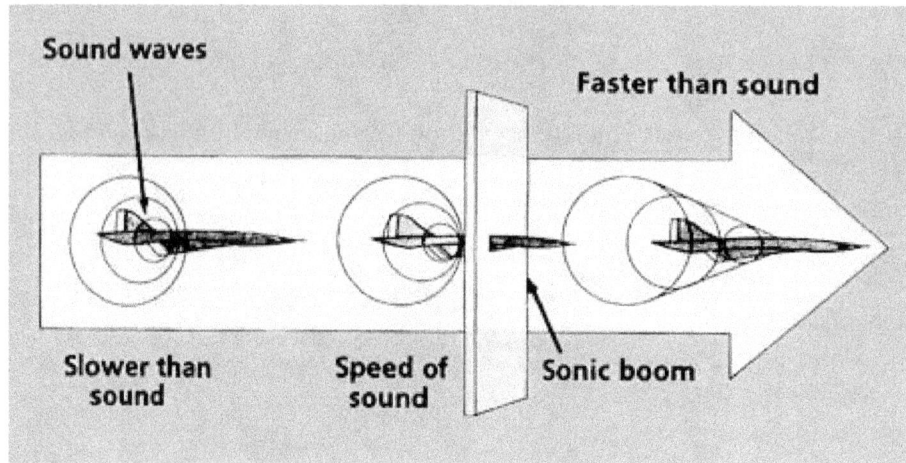

Sonic Boom

Speed of light in air = 3 * 108 m/s

Speed of sound in air = 333 m/s

This clearly states that sound travels a lower speed than that of light in air. This is a reason why at the time of lightening, the light is visible instantly while the sound of the thunder reaches our ears after a few seconds.

Sound can bounce off a solid or a liquid. Some materials like metals and walls are called Good Reflectors of Sound as they do not absorb the sound while others like clothes and sponge are called Bad Reflectors of Sound as they absorb the sound easily.

Laws of Reflection of Sound

The incident sound wave, the reflected sound wave and the normal, all lie in the same plane.

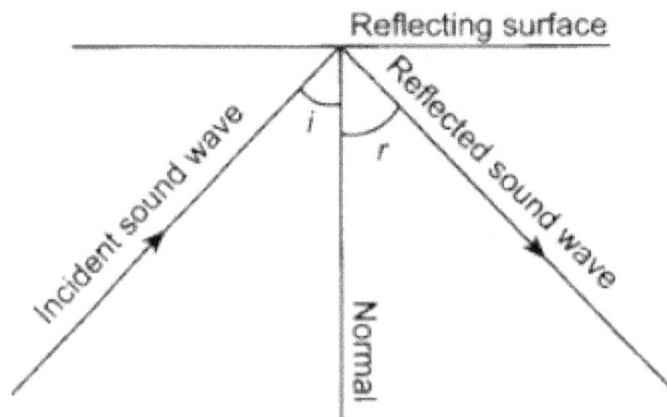

Laws of Reflection of Sound

The angle of incident of incident sound wave is equal to the angle of reflection formed by the reflected sound wave, that is, i = r

Echo

When we hear the same sound again and again in a medium it is called Echo. The sound or echo persists in our brain for 0.1 seconds. This means that the difference between sound and its echo should be at least 0.1 seconds. It is produced as a result of reflection of sound through a medium. If sound reflects more than once we may hear multiple echoes.

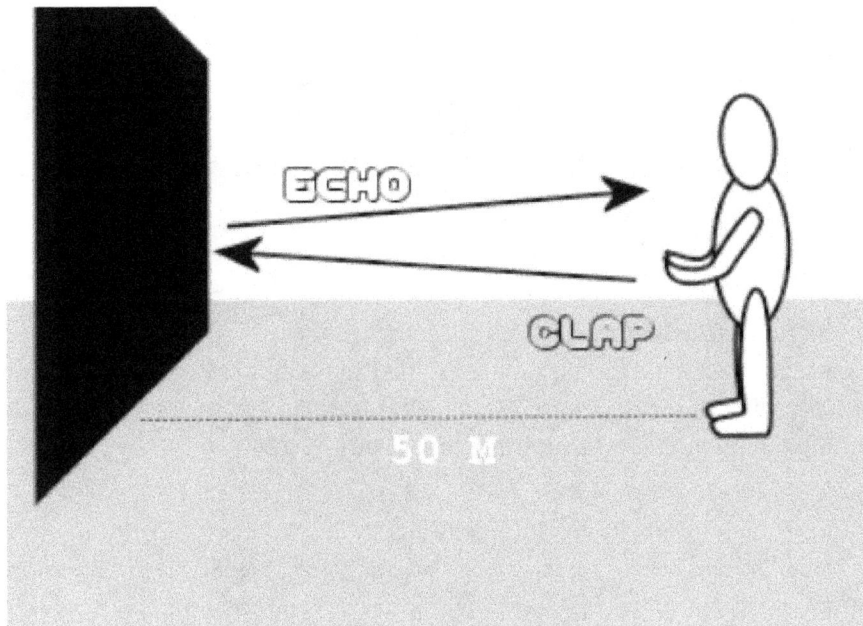

echo

Echo

Reverberation

It is the persistence of a sound after a sound is produced. A reverberation is created when a sound signal is reflected multiple of times until it reaches a sound wave that cannot be heard by human ears. Auditoriums and big halls often have to deal with reverberation. That is why the roofs are made up of soundproof materials like Flipboard and the chairs in the halls are also made up of fabrics that can absorb sound.

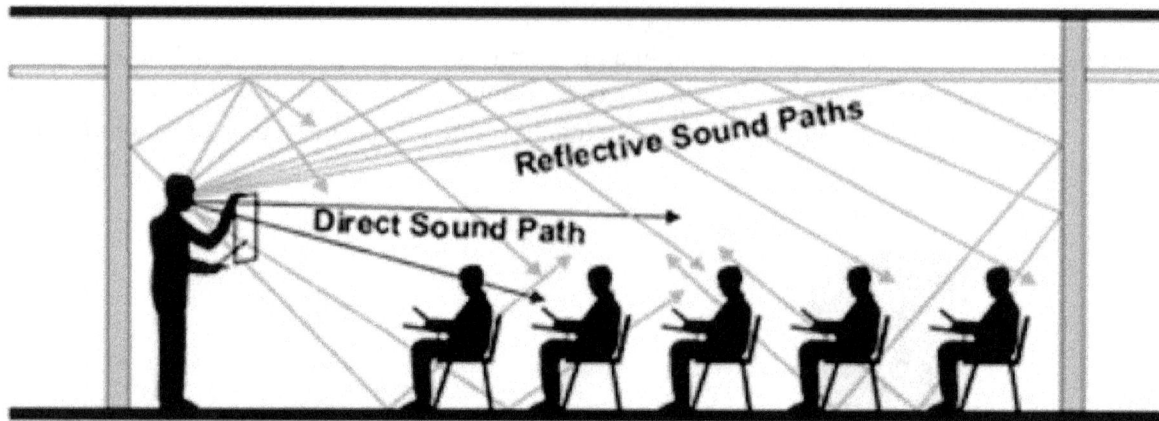

Reverberation

Advantages of Multiple Reflection of Sound

Horns, trumpets, loudhailers or megaphones are designed in such a way that sound can travel in a particular direction only without spreading out everywhere. This makes it easier for the audience to listen to the speaker. All these instruments work on the phenomena of multiple reflections of sound.

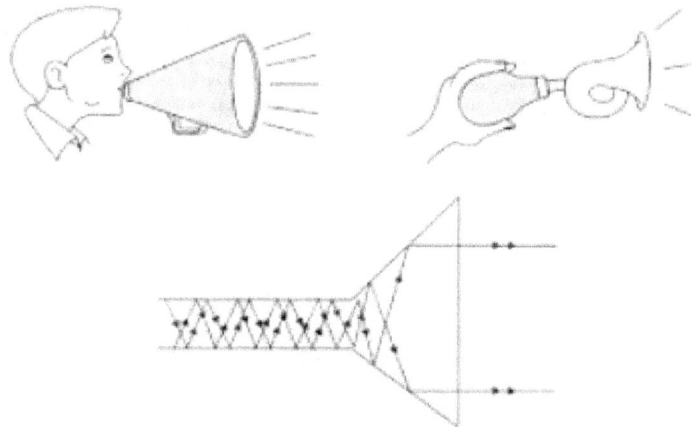

Multiple Reflections through a horn and megaphone

The multiple reflections in a stethoscope tube make it possible for the doctors to listen to a patient's heartbeat.

Concert halls are generally covered so that sound can reflect through it and reach the wider audience.

The range of sound – on the basis of the range of frequency of a sound, it is categorized into ultrasound and infrasound.

Human auditory range is between 20 Hz and 20000 Hz.

InfrasoundUltrasound

Infrasound refers to the sound with frequency lower than 20 Hz which can't be heard by humans.

Ultrasound refers to the sound with frequency higher than the upper limit (20 kHz) of frequencies audible to normal human ears.

Infrasound is used to stabilize myopia in young kids.

Ultrasound is commonly used to find flaws in materials to measure the thickness of objects, to fund physical abnormalities in various parts of human body, as well as in the form of a sound ranging device called Sonar.

Infrasound is influenced by the atmosphere so it can be used to monitor the activities of the atmosphere.

Ultrasound is not influenced by any such factors.

In particular, natural disasters such as volcanic eruptions, earthquakes etc can be forecasted by monitoring the infrasonic waves.

In particular, ultrasound is also used in micro welding. The weld is produced by the application of higher frequency vibratory energy as the parts are held together with force.

Range of Infrasound and Ultrasounds

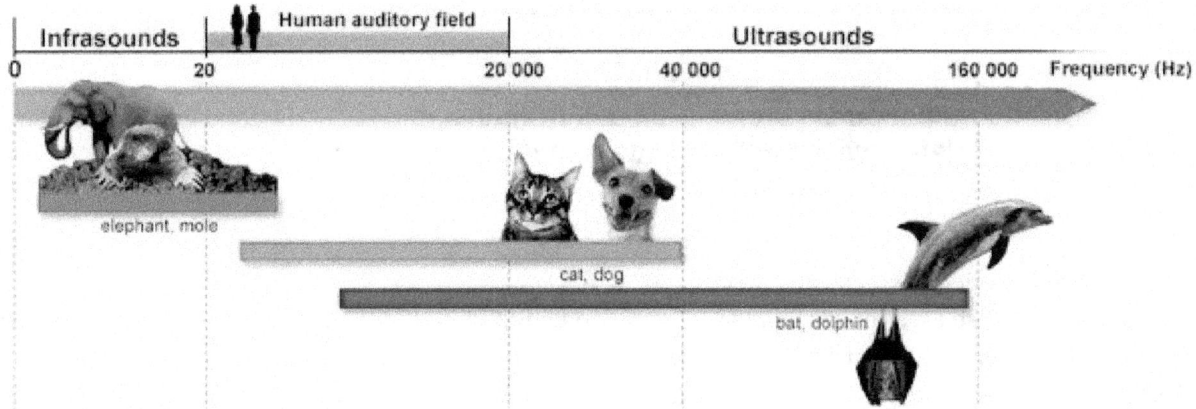

range of infra and ultra sound

Hearing Aid- The Hearing Aid contains a microphone which receives the sound from the outer atmosphere and converts it into electrical energy. This electrical energy is passed through an amplifier which amplifies the sound and then moves it to a speaker. The speaker then converts the electrical signal into sound waves and sends it to the ear and provides a clear hearing.

Applications of Ultrasound

The ultrasound waves are the sound waves with high frequency. Due to this, they can travel long distances despite any obstacles between their paths.

The ultrasound waves are used in clearing parts of objects that are hard to reach such as a spiral tube or electronic components. In order to clean the objects, they are put in a solution, then the ultrasonic waves are passed through the solution. As a result, the dust particles on the object get detached and fall off them.

Ultrasound waves can recognize tiny cracks in metallic objects that are used in the manufacture of large structures, buildings and scientific equipment. The presence of such cracks can lower the strength of these structures and machines. Hence, the ultrasound waves are passed through the metallic objects and detectors are used to detect the waves that pass through the cracks. If a crack is present the ultrasound waves would reflect back.

Defect or flaw

Ultrasound

Detectors

Metal Block

Ultrasound is reflected back from the
defective locations inside a metal block.

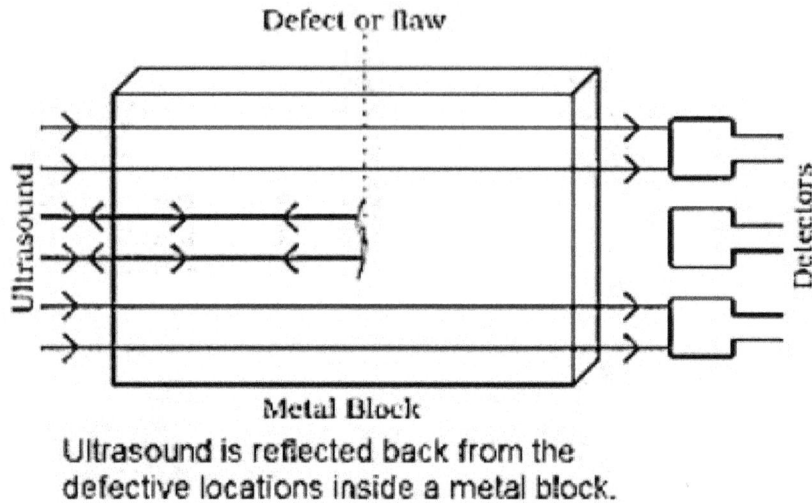

Ultrasound waves can detect cracks in a metal

Ultrasonic waves are also used in a medical process called Echocardiography. In this process, the ultrasound waves are passed through various parts of the heart in order to form the images of the organ.

Ultrasonic waves are also used in a procedure called Ultrasonography. In this procedure, the ultrasonic waves are passed through the internal organs of the body in order to get their image. In this way, the doctors can find out the cause of a disease or any abnormalities in the organs. The ultrasound waves travel through the tissues of the body and as soon as the density of the tissue changes they reflect back. The reflected waves are then converted into electrical signals which form the images of the internal organs.

Ultrasound waves are also used to break the kidney stones.

SONAR – Sound Navigation and Ranging

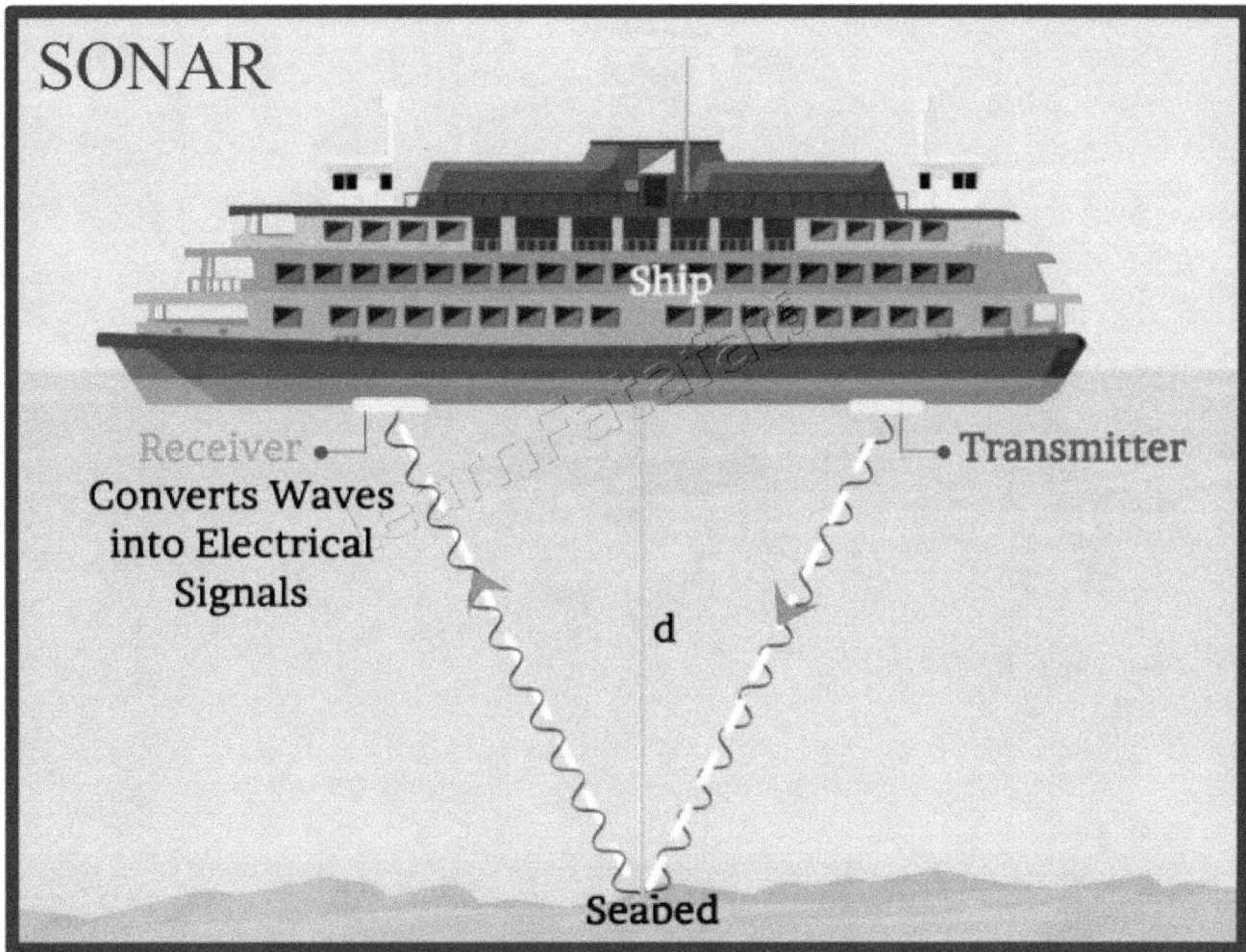

Sonar

This device is used to find the distance, direction and speed of objects that are present under the water. It uses Ultrasonic waves to do so.

The Sonar consists of two main devices – The transmitter and the detector (or receiver). The main function of the transmitter is the production and transmission of the Ultrasonic waves in water.

As these waves travel underwater, they, when hit by an object, reflect back to the detector. The detector then converts these sound waves into electrical signals which are then interpreted.

The distance of the object is calculated with the help of the speed of sound in water and time taken by the way to reach the detector. This process is called Echo Ranging.

Uses of Sonar

Finding the depth of a water body such as sea

Detecting the presence of underwater objects like submarines, hills, icebergs and ships

How do bats search their prey?

Bats generate Ultrasonic waves. As these waves hit an object, they get reflected back to the bat's ears. The bats can understand the nature of reflection of these waves and then can decide the position of the object over their prey.

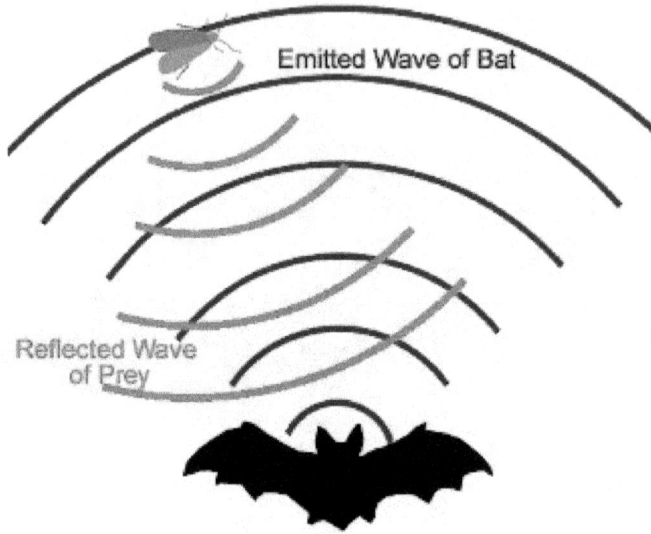

Enter Caption

Ultrasonic waves generated by bats

The Human Ear

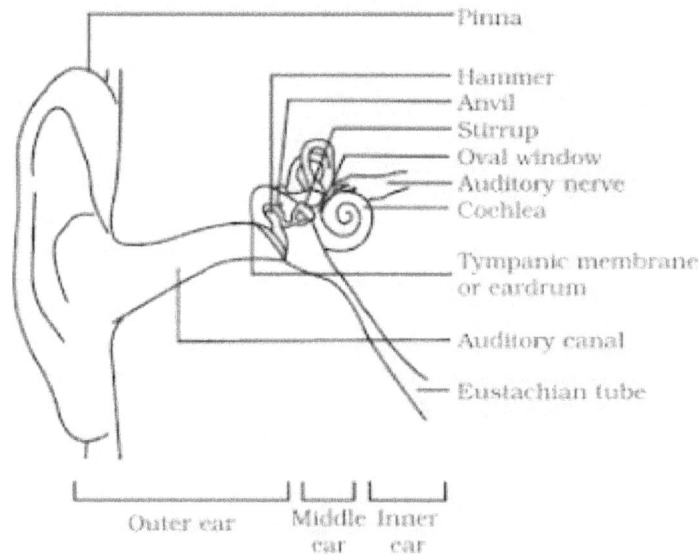

Structure of Human Ear

Our ears allow us to receive audible frequencies in our surroundings. They then convert these sounds into electrical signals which are then passed through a special nerve called the auditory nerve to our brain. The brain that interprets these signals and responds accordingly.

Pinna – The outer part of the ear that gathers sound from the environment.

Auditory Canal – Sound collected from the surroundings passes through the Auditory Canal.

Eardrum or Tympanic Membrane – It is located at the end of the auditory canal. The eardrum when receives a compression moves inwards because of increased pressure. Similarly, when it receives refraction it moves outwards due to a decrease in pressure. As a result, it starts to vibrate inwards and outwards on receiving a sound wave.

The Middle Ear – It consists of three bones (hammer, anvil and stirrup). These bones amplify the vibrations produced by the eardrum. These vibrations are then passed onto the inner ear by the middle ear.

Cochlea – It is located in the inner ear. It converts the vibrations into electrical signals which are then carried to the brain by the auditory nerve.

Thanks for reading this book . I hope it is useful to you all .So thankyou once again to all of you

CPSIA information can be obtained
at www.ICGtesting.com
Printed in the USA
BVHW020250030623
665300BV00004B/172